Reading
Skills

Grade 6

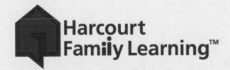

Harcourt Family Learning™

© 2004 by Flash Kids
Adapted from *Comprehension Skills Complete Classroom Library*
by Linda Ward Beech, Tara McCarthy, and Donna Townsend
© 2001 by Harcourt Achieve
Licensed under special arrangement with Harcourt Achieve.

Illustrator: Ethan Long

ISBN-13: 978-1-4114-0077-1

Please submit all inquiries to FlashKids@bn.com

Manufactured in China

Lot #:

30 31 29

07/17

Flash Kids
A Division of Barnes & Noble
122 Fifth Avenue
New York, NY 10011

Dear Parent,

The ability to read well is an important part of your child's development. This book is designed to help your child become a better reader. The wide range of high-interest stories will hold your child's attention and help develop his or her proficiency in reading. Each of the six units focuses on a different reading comprehension skill: finding facts, detecting a sequence, learning new vocabulary through context, identifying the main idea, drawing conclusions, and making inferences. Mastering these skills will ensure that your child has the necessary tools needed for a lifetime love of reading.

Unit 1 contains activities to fine-tune your child's ability to spot facts in a story—a necessary skill for understanding a reading selection. This unit is filled with stories to test your child's understanding of how to identify facts in a story. The focus is on specific details that tell who, what, when, where, and how.

Reading for sequence means identifying the order of events in a story or the steps in a process, and understanding the relationship of one event or step to other events or steps. Unit 2 contains stories that will test your child's understanding of the order of events in a story.

Unit 3 teaches your child how to use context to learn new words. When practicing using context, your child must use all the words in a reading selection to understand the unfamiliar words. This important skill helps a reader understand words and concepts by learning how language is used to express meaning. Mastering this skill ensures that your child will become a successful independent reader.

One of the keys to learning to read well is being able to differentiate between the main point of a reading selection and the supporting details. Unit 4 will help your child learn to recognize the main idea of a story.

Drawing a conclusion is a complex reading skill because a conclusion is not stated in a reading selection. Your child must learn to put together the details from the information as if they were clues to a puzzle. The conclusion must be supported by the details in the reading selection. Unit 5 contains stories to help your child learn to draw conclusions about the passages in the book.

To make an inference, your child must consider all the facts in a reading selection. Then he or she must put together those facts and what is already known to make a reasonable inference about something that is not stated in the selection. Making an inference requires the reader to go beyond the information in the text. Unit 6 will help your child learn how to make inferences.

To help your child get the most from this workbook, encourage your child to read each reading selection slowly and carefully. Explain the purpose of each unit to your child so that he or she has a better understanding of how it will help his or her reading skills. There's an answer key at the end of this workbook. Your child can check the answer key to see which questions he or she got right and wrong. Go back to the questions your child answered incorrectly and go over them again to see why he or she picked the incorrect answer. Completing the activities in this workbook will get your child on the right track to becoming an excellent reader. Continue your child's educational development at home with these fun activities:

- Enlist your child's help when writing grocery lists.
- When preparing a meal, have your child read the recipe aloud.
- Provide entertaining reading selections for your child. Have a discussion about what he or she has read.
- Instead of reading a bedtime story to your child, have your child read a bedtime story to you!
- Write down the directions to a project, such as a gardening project or an arts and crafts project, for your child to read.
- Give your child a fun reading passage and ask him or her to draw a picture about it.
- Ask your child to read road signs and billboards that you encounter during car trips.
- Leave cute notes on the refrigerator or your child's pillow.
- Have your child write and mail a letter to a loved one.
- Ask your child to read the directions for a board game, and then play the game together.
- Bring your child to the library or bookstore so that he or she can choose which great book to read next.

Table of Contents

What Are Facts?

Facts are sometimes called details. They are small pieces of information. Facts can appear in true stories, such as those in the newspaper. They can also appear in legends and other stories that people make up.

How to Read for Facts

You can find facts by asking yourself questions. Ask *who*, and your answer will be a fact about a person. Ask *what*, and your answer will be a fact about a thing. Ask *where*, and your answer will be a fact about a place. Ask *when*, and your answer will be a fact about a time. Ask *how many* or *how much*, and your answer will be a fact about a number or an amount.

Try It!

Read this story and look for facts as you read. Ask yourself *when* and *who*.

The First Airplane Flight

Wilbur and Orville Wright read everything they could find about flying machines. They began building their own airplane in 1900. They carefully tested every part of the airplane. Finally on a cold, windy day in December 1903, they flew their plane for the first time. Orville was the pilot as the plane lifted into the air. It stayed in the air for only 12 seconds and traveled just 120 feet the first time. After three more tries that same day, the plane's longest trip was almost a full minute and more than 850 feet.

Did you find these facts when you read the paragraph? Write the facts on the lines below.

◆ When did the Wrights fly for the first time?

Fact: _____

◆ Who was the pilot?

Fact: _____

Practice Finding Facts

Below are some practice questions. The first two are already answered. Answer the third one on your own.

_C_   **1.** How long was the plane's longest trip?

    A. 120 feet   **c.** 850 feet

    B. 85 feet   **D.** 12 feet

Look at the question and answers again. *How long* is asking for a number. There are many numbers in the paragraph, but you are looking for one that describes the plane's longest trip. Read the paragraph until you find the words *longest trip*. You should find this sentence: "After three more tries that same day, the plane's longest trip was almost a full minute and more than 850 feet." So **c** is the correct answer. Answer **A** is also a fact from the story, but it describes the first trip, not the longest one.

_D_   **2.** The Wright brothers first flew their plane in

    A. summer   **c.** fall

    B. spring   **D.** winter

Look at the question. The first answer you might think of is a place, but the possible answers are seasons. Search the story for words about seasons or time of year. You should find this sentence: "Finally on a cold, windy day in December 1903, they flew their plane for the first time." The correct answer is *winter*. The answer uses different words, but the fact is the same.

Now it's your turn to practice. Answer the next question by writing the letter of the correct answer on the line.

_____ **3.** The Wrights first started working on their airplane in

    A. 1903   **c.** 1908

    B. 1900   **D.** 1809

Read each story. After each story you will answer questions about the facts in the story. Remember, a fact is something that you know is true.

Scarecrows Then and Now

Birds have always been a problem for farmers. They like to eat the seeds in farmers' fields. As soon as a farmer plants seeds, the birds arrive for dinner. Often these birds are crows.

Farmers try to get rid of their unwanted visitors by making scarecrows. A scarecrow is supposed to scare away crows and other birds. The first scarecrows were made hundreds of years ago. They were sticks stuck in the ground with big rags tied to the top. When the wind blew, the rags flapped and frightened the birds.

As time went on, farmers began making better scarecrows. They nailed a second stick across the top of the one in the ground. Now the scarecrows had arms and could wear old shirts. When farmers stuffed the shirts with straw, the scarecrows began to look like real people. Some even had faces.

_____ **1.** Birds like to eat
     A. fields   **C.** rags
     B. seeds   **D.** sticks

_____ **2.** A scarecrow is supposed to scare away
     A. gardens   **C.** birds
     B. seeds   **D.** sticks

_____ **3.** The first scarecrows were made from sticks and
     A. rags   **C.** rugs
     B. plants   **D.** hats

_____ **4.** Later, farmers filled scarecrows with
     A. cotton   **C.** straw
     B. air   **D.** string

_____ **5.** Scarecrows flapped because of the
     A. arms   **C.** birds
     B. noise   **D.** wind

When farmers began using modern machines, they didn't need scarecrows anymore. The new farm machines were big and made a lot of noise. They scared the birds away quite well.

In the 1960s people became interested in folk art such as scarecrows. Suddenly scarecrows were popular again. People wanted them for their yards and vegetable gardens. Even people in cities bought scarecrows for their porches.

Today some artists make scarecrows to sell. They use natural materials such as sticks and straw for the bodies. However, these new scarecrows are often dressed in fancy clothes. Some wear sunglasses, belts, or scarves. Some scarecrows may have beads, flowers, and purses.

_____ **6.** People didn't need scarecrows because they had
- **A.** clothes
- **B.** machines
- **C.** workers
- **D.** crows

_____ **7.** In the 1960s people thought that scarecrows were
- **A.** folk art
- **B.** sunglasses
- **C.** farm workers
- **D.** fine art

_____ **8.** People put scarecrows on porches and in
- **A.** machines
- **B.** cities
- **C.** yards
- **D.** parks

_____ **9.** Today some artists make scarecrows for
- **A.** sale
- **B.** beads
- **C.** sail
- **D.** style

_____ **10.** Scarecrows sometimes have beads, flowers, and
- **A.** ties
- **B.** shoes
- **C.** pins
- **D.** purses

Merry-Go-Rounds

The organ starts, and its music fills the air. The horses slowly begin to move. Riders hold tightly as their colorful horses go up and down and around and around. These riders are on a carousel. *Carousel* is another word for *merry-go-round*.

Carousels have a long history. In the 1400s soldiers in France liked to play a ball game on horseback. The soldiers had to throw and catch while their horses were moving. The French invented a way to help the soldiers practice for the game.

This invention was the first carousel. It was different from modern carousels. The biggest difference was that the horses were real! They turned the carousel as they moved in a circle. Years later, people began using carousels for fun. By the 1800s carousel horses were no longer real. Carousels were run by motors.

_____ **1.** *Merry-go-round* is another word for
      A. ferris wheel   **C.** roller coaster
      B. moving horse   **D.** carousel

_____ **2.** The music for carousels comes from
      A. riders   **C.** pianos
      B. organs   **D.** radios

_____ **3.** The first carousel was made to help players
      A. fight wars   **C.** ride horses
      B. invent tricks   **D.** practice skills

_____ **4.** The horses on the first carousels were
      A. real   **C.** painted
      B. wood   **D.** motors

_____ **5.** The first people to use a carousel were
      A. inventors   **C.** soldiers
      B. sailors   **D.** children

Once there were 10,000 merry-go-rounds in the United States. Most were made in Pennsylvania and New York. Workers carved and painted the carousel horses. Some horses had fine saddles and roses around their necks. Others had a wild look in their shiny glass eyes. No two horses were the same.

Today there are fewer than 300 merry-go-rounds in North America. Some of these rides are now treasured as historic places.

One of the nation's oldest merry-go-rounds is in Oak Bluffs, Massachusetts. This carousel is called the Flying Horses. It was built around 1880. Riders on the Flying Horses can have some extra fun. As the merry-go-round spins, riders try to grab rings from a post on the wall. The person who gets the most rings is the winner. The reward is a free ride.

_____ **6.** No two carousel horses were
   A. bright   **C.** carved
   B. wild   **D.** alike

_____ **7.** One state where carousels were made was
   A. Massachusetts   **C.** France
   B. Pennsylvania   **D.** Oak Bluffs

_____ **8.** Some carousels are now considered to be
   A. too fast   **C.** historic
   B. dangerous   **D.** too small

_____ **9.** One of America's oldest carousels is called the
   A. Oak Bluffs   **C.** Fighting Horses
   B. Flying Horses   **D.** New York

_____ **10.** A free ride on this merry-go-round is given as a
   A. prize   **C.** ring
   B. horse   **D.** win

How to Win a Prize

There are all kinds of contests. Have you ever heard of the Apple Seed Popping Contest? It's held on the first weekend in October in Lincoln, Nebraska. How does it work? Line up with everybody else. Take a fresh apple, and squeeze it hard in your fist. If your apple seeds pop the farthest, you're a winner!

Do you like food contests? Every August in Fulton, Kentucky, there's a banana contest. If you eat the most bananas within a set time, you win some more bananas. If you like milk, go to Los Angeles, California, in September. Sign up for the Milk Drinking Contest. If you win, you get a ribbon.

In Albany, Oregon, anyone between the ages of 5 and 12 can enter the Bubble Gum Blowing Contest. You'll win some books if you blow the first bubble, the biggest bubble, or the bubble that lasts the longest.

_____ **1.** The Apple Seed Popping Contest is held in
      A. California   **C.** August
      B. October   **D.** Albany

_____ **2.** To win the Apple Seed Popping Contest, you must
      A. be under 16   **C.** pop seeds the farthest
      B. line up the seeds   **D.** squeeze the fresh apple

_____ **3.** The winner of the banana contest gets
      A. a set time   **C.** more bananas
      B. a ribbon   **D.** a trip to Fulton

_____ **4.** People who like milk could sign up for a contest in
      A. Los Angeles   **C.** Oregon
      B. Nebraska   **D.** Kentucky

_____ **5.** The person who blows the biggest bubble wins
      A. gum   **C.** books
      B. food   **D.** bikes

Some contests require a special animal. In May bring your chicken to the Chicken Flying Meet in Rio Grande, Ohio. Put your chicken on the launchpad. At the signal, give it a little push. If your chicken flies the farthest, you win a cash prize.

People 14 and under can enter the Greasy Pig Scramble in Dothan, Alabama. The pigs are greased with peanut oil. You have to catch the greasy pig and hold on to it until it crosses the finish line. If you win, you get the pig.

If you have a pet crab, you can enter it in the World Championship Crab Race in California. The International Frog Jumping and Racing Contest is held in Louisiana. Winners of both contests get medals. Petaluma, California, holds an Ugly Dog Contest. The winners receive medals and are invited to come back next year for the Ugliest Dog Contest.

_____ **6.** In some contests, you need a pet that is
     A. slow   **C.** afraid
     B. prized   **D.** unusual

_____ **7.** The Chicken Flying Meet is in
     A. Ohio   **C.** California
     B. Alabama   **D.** Louisiana

_____ **8.** In the Dothan, Alabama, contest you have to
     A. use peanuts   **C.** count pigs
     B. hold on   **D.** push chickens

_____ **9.** Louisiana has a special contest for
     A. frogs   **C.** crabs
     B. dogs   **D.** pigs

_____**10.** The Ugliest Dog Contest is for dogs that
     A. are not strange   **C.** won the year before
     B. live in Ohio   **D.** like to get medals

The Birth of an Island

It was a gray November day in 1963. A fishing boat rocked in the Atlantic Ocean off the southern coast of Iceland. Suddenly a great black cloud burst from the water. Loud noises rumbled from the ocean. The ship's captain sent out a radio call. Something very unusual was happening!

In the next three hours, scientists and reporters arrived at the scene. By now the cloud was 12,000 feet high. Huge explosions sent ash, dust, and hot rocks into the air. The watchers could see something just under the water's surface.

By that night a new mountain had pushed itself up from the boiling sea. The mountain continued to rise during the next days. It also grew wider. A fiery island was growing in the Atlantic. It was caused by a volcano in the ocean.

_____ **1.** The fishing boat was off the coast of
     A. Ireland   **C.** Iceland
     B. Greenland   **D.** November

_____ **2.** The ship's captain used a
     A. radio   **C.** telephone
     B. light   **D.** surface

_____ **3.** The explosions sent up ash, dust, and hot
     A. food   **C.** ice
     B. rocks   **D.** fish

_____ **4.** The mountain grew into
     A. an island   **C.** a valley
     B. a nation   **D.** an iceberg

_____ **5.** The explosion came from
     A. an island   **C.** an earthquake
     B. a volcano   **D.** a fishing boat

The new island continued to grow for two years. It finally stopped in August of 1965. It was 550 feet high. It was more than 1 mile long and about 6 miles around.

The people of Iceland named the new island Surtsey. This name comes from an old myth. In the story Surtur was a mighty fire giant. People thought that Surtsey was also a giant by the time it stopped growing.

Scientists are very interested in Surtsey. It is the first new island to appear in the North Atlantic in 200 years. Scientists want to learn more about how this happened. They are also studying how plant life begins on a new island. Another thing scientists want to know is how long Surtsey will last. They wonder whether the island will be destroyed by the same volcano that created it.

_____ **6.** The new island became quiet in
       A. 1956   **C.** the old story
       B. 1963   **D.** 1965

_____ **7.** Surtur was a fire giant in an old
       A. tale   **C.** snow
       B. island   **D.** volcano

_____ **8.** In the myth Surtur was
       A. cloudy   **C.** powerful
       B. weak   **D.** peaceful

_____ **9.** Scientists are studying
       A. plant life   **C.** people
       B. dead fish   **D.** animal life

_____ **10.** Scientists also want to know how long Surtsey will
       A. return   **C.** burn
       B. remain   **D.** flood

How to Box the Gnat

All over the country, many Americans are learning to "dip for the oyster," "box the gnat," and "wring the dishrag." These are special names for different movements in square dances.

A square-dance party may be called by many names. Such a party may be called a hog wrassle, a hoedown, a barndance, or a shindig. All square dances are alike in certain ways. Four couples line up and face each other. A caller chants or sings directions. The dancers shuffle, glide, or run while people clap.

Pioneers in New England started these dances. As people moved westward and southward, new movements were added. In the Midwest, dancers created the "grand right and left." In the far West, cowboys lifted their partners off the ground during "the swing."

_____ **1.** The dance movements have special

     A. squares   **C.** shindigs

     B. names   **D.** boxes

_____ **2.** A hoedown is a kind of

     A. party   **C.** step

     B. sport   **D.** tool

_____ **3.** The caller gives

     A. parties   **C.** squares

     B. directions   **D.** barndances

_____ **4.** Square dancing started in

     A. the Far West   **C.** New England

     B. the South   **D.** the Midwest

_____ **5.** In "the swing," men lifted their partners

     A. to the right   **C.** off the ground

     B. to the left   **D.** grand right and left

Square dancing comes from dances done long ago in England. People there did *country dances*. In one country dance, dancers formed a circle. This dance was called a round. Another country dance was the longways. In this one, two long lines of dancers faced one another. A popular longways is called the Virginia reel.

Around the year 1900, square dancing was dying out. Dancers liked the new *couple dancing* better. In the 1940s, people became interested in the songs and dances the pioneers enjoyed. Square dancing became popular again. The interest in square dancing is still growing, but it's not easy to learn some of those movements! Square-dance contests award ribbons or badges to the winners. If you're invited to a hog wrassle, get ready for music, action, and fun.

_____ **6.** In a round
     A. a circle is formed   **C.** people wrestled
     B. a longways is danced   **D.** people dance in Virginia

_____ **7.** The Virginia reel is a
     A. longways   **C.** couple dance
     B. square   **D.** new name

_____ **8.** Between 1900 and 1940, couple dancing became
     A. impossible   **C.** a round
     B. popular   **D.** a longways

_____ **9.** Square dancing started again when people became
     A. interested in history   **C.** tired of couples
     B. better Americans   **D.** buyers of clothing

_____ **10.** In a square-dance contest, people earn
     A. boots   **C.** difficult movements
     B. music   **D.** ribbons or badges

Home Sweet Home

How would you like to come home after a long day, open the door, and walk into an elephant? That's what you would do if you lived in Elephant House in Margate, New Jersey. The elephant-shaped house was built in 1881 by James Lafferty. In 1962, Herbert Green built a chicken-shaped house.

Sarah Winchester tried to build a ghost-proof house in San Jose, California. Workers built fake chimneys, doors that open onto blank walls, and stairs that lead nowhere. Many rooms were torn down and then rebuilt in a new way to confuse the ghosts. It took 38 years to complete the house!

Some houses are built of strange materials. A house in Pigeon Cove, Massachusetts, is built from more than 100,000 newspapers. In Canada, George Plumb built a house entirely out of bottles.

_____ **1.** The elephant-shaped house was built in
     A. 1881   **C.** 1922
     B. 1884   **D.** 1962

_____ **2.** Herbert Green's house is shaped like
     A. a chicken   **C.** an elephant
     B. a door   **D.** a pigeon

_____ **3.** Sarah Winchester built a house in
     A. Massachusetts   **C.** New Jersey
     B. California   **D.** Oklahoma

_____ **4.** Winchester tried to build a house that was
     A. a castle   **C.** rebuilt
     B. fool-proof   **D.** ghost-proof

_____ **5.** George Plumb's house is built of
     A. newspapers   **C.** chimneys
     B. aluminum cans   **D.** bottles

Some homes stand for great wealth and power. The Palace of Alhambra in Spain is one of the most beautiful homes in the world. The man who built it loved water. A stream runs through all 9 acres of the palace. In each room there is a small pool of sparkling water.

Wealthy Americans design dream houses too. In 1895, Cornelius Vanderbilt moved into a house named the Breakers. He called it his summer cottage. It cost $10 million to build and has walls trimmed with gold. This "summer cottage" could hold 60 guests comfortably.

Dream houses don't have to be expensive. A man named Baldasera built a house with 90 rooms for about $300 by digging under the earth. Baldasera worked alone. He spent about 40 years completing his underground house.

_____ **6.** The Palace of Alhambra covers
      A. 40 years   **C.** $10 million
      B. 9 acres   **D.** 90 rooms

_____ **7.** The builder of the Palace of Alhambra loved
      A. water   **C.** wealth and power
      B. chances to swim   **D.** pools with lights

_____ **8.** Vanderbilt designed the Breakers to be his summer
      A. museum   **C.** home
      B. camp   **D.** dream

_____ **9.** Baldasera built his home
      A. in Spain   **C.** without much money
      B. at the Breakers   **D.** in a mountain

_____**10.** To build his house, Baldasera needed much
      A. help   **C.** time
      B. water   **D.** money

Nature Paints a Turtle

A dozen small turtles slide off a rock and slip into the pond. These turtles look as if an artist had painted them. Pale yellow stripes cross their upper shells, and a red border circles the edge. More red and yellow stripes are on the turtles' heads, and just behind each eye is another yellow spot.

These eastern painted turtles live in slow-moving rivers, marshy areas, and ponds. They like to be in places where rocks and fallen trees project from the water. The turtles like to climb out onto the rocks or dead trees to sleep in the warm sunlight. If something frightens them, they slide quickly into the water.

Eastern painted turtles keep regular schedules. They nap at certain times, and they eat at certain times. In the late morning and the late afternoon, the turtles search for food.

_____ **1.** Eastern painted turtles are mainly red and
        A. green   **C.** blue
        B. orange   **D.** yellow

_____ **2.** These turtles live near rivers that are
        A. deep   **C.** slow
        B. warm   **D.** fast

_____ **3.** The turtles like to sleep
        A. in the sunlight   **C.** inside trees
        B. under the water   **D.** while eating

_____ **4.** The turtles move quickly when they are
        A. hungry   **C.** sleepy
        B. certain   **D.** frightened

_____ **5.** In the late afternoon, the turtles
        A. climb on rocks   **C.** slide into the water
        B. search for food   **D.** go swimming

Painted turtles eat almost anything they can find in their water homes. They feed on plants, insects, crayfish, and snails. Since young turtles need to grow fast, they usually eat more animal food than older turtles do. When winter comes, the turtles dig into the underwater mud and sleep there until warm weather returns.

Once a year, in the early summer, the females crawl to dry land. There they dig nests and lay their eggs. In about 10 weeks, the young turtles hatch, and the real battle for life begins. As the turtles creep toward the water, many of them are caught and eaten by hungry raccoons, snakes, and bullfrogs.

Some varieties of young eastern painted turtles stay in their nests all through their first summer, fall, and winter. When they come out the following spring, they are larger, stronger, and quicker. Then they have a better chance of escaping their enemies.

_____ **6.** To turtles, crayfish and snails are
       A. insects   **C.** enemies
       B. food   **D.** friends

_____ **7.** Animal food helps turtles
       A. grow quickly   **C.** eat more
       B. swim faster   **D.** sleep longer

_____ **8.** In the winter the turtles live
       A. close to water   **C.** under the mud
       B. on dry land   **D.** in warm homes

_____ **9.** Little turtles can be caught as they
       A. dig their nests   **C.** crawl toward water
       B. lay their eggs   **D.** hunt snakes

_____**10.** Some varieties of turtles remain in their nests
       A. until they lay eggs   **C.** for about 10 weeks
       B. for almost a year   **D.** to hide from raccoons

Hunter in the Sky

Stargazing takes imagination. People who love stargazing see the stars as shining spots in a dot-to-dot drawing game. They imagine lines that connect groups of stars called constellations. A constellation is a group of stars that looks like a person, an animal, or an object.

The constellation Orion is known as the hunter, after a hero from ancient Greek myths. To find Orion, first find the Big Dipper. The Big Dipper looks like a huge cup with a long handle. After you find the Big Dipper, turn around. There's Orion! He is outlined by four bright stars that form two triangles. The tips of the triangles seem to come together. Where they meet, there are three more bright stars. These form Orion's belt. Some fainter stars appear to hang from the belt. These are Orion's sword.

_____ **1.** When looking at a constellation, people try to imagine

    A. lines   **C.** spots

    B. games   **D.** groups

_____ **2.** Groups of stars are called

    A. stargazers   **C.** constellations

    B. ancient myths   **D.** connections

_____ **3.** Orion is named after a Greek

    A. object   **C.** animal

    B. story   **D.** hero

_____ **4.** The four bright stars in Orion form

    A. a big cup   **C.** a long handle

    B. two triangles   **D.** an animal

_____ **5.** Three bright stars form Orion's

    A. shoulder   **C.** belt

    B. sword   **D.** spear

Different kinds of stars are in the constellation Orion. The star Betelgeuse makes Orion's right shoulder. *Betelgeuse* is an Arabic word that means "shoulder of the giant." The star itself is so huge that it is called a supergiant. Its diameter is 400 times greater than that of our Sun. Betelgeuse is considered a cool star. It is probably not as hot as our Sun.

Rigel is the star that makes Orion's left foot. *Rigel* is the Arabic word for *foot*. Rigel is much brighter than Betelgeuse because it is much hotter. It's more than three times as hot as our Sun. However, Rigel is just a baby in size compared to Betelgeuse.

A large, misty area near Orion's sword is called a nebula. It is a mass of shining gas and dust. The gases whirl together and may form new stars. As the new stars begin to shine, Orion will be brighter than ever.

_____ **6.** Betelgeuse makes
    A. Arabic words   **C.** different stars
    B. Orion's shoulder   **D.** huge sizes

_____ **7.** Betelgeuse is much larger than
    A. our Sun   **C.** a diameter
    B. a supergiant   **D.** any nebula

_____ **8.** Rigel is brighter than Betelgeuse because it is
    A. bigger   **C.** hotter
    B. smaller   **D.** cooler

_____ **9.** Near Orion's sword is
    A. a cool star   **C.** a new star
    B. strange material   **D.** a nebula

_____ **10.** Orion may shine brighter
    A. when Rigel explodes   **C.** as dust shines
    B. as new stars shine   **D.** as dust forms

Writing Roundup

Read the story below. Think about the facts. Then answer the questions in complete sentences.

Have you ever seen the Statue of Liberty? It is a tall figure of a robed woman holding a torch. She stands proudly on Liberty Island in New York Harbor. The statue is a symbol of freedom for the United States. It was given as a gift to the United States by France in 1884.

The statue is one of the largest ever built. It stands 151 feet high from its base to the top of the torch. When the statue was shipped to America, it could not be sent in one piece. Instead it was taken apart and packed in 214 separate crates.

1. What is the Statue of Liberty?

_____

_____

2. Who gave the statue to the United States?

_____

_____

3. How tall is the statue?

_____

_____

Prewriting

Think of an idea you might write about, such as a building in your town or a place you once visited. Write the idea in the center of the idea web below. Then fill out the rest of the web with facts.

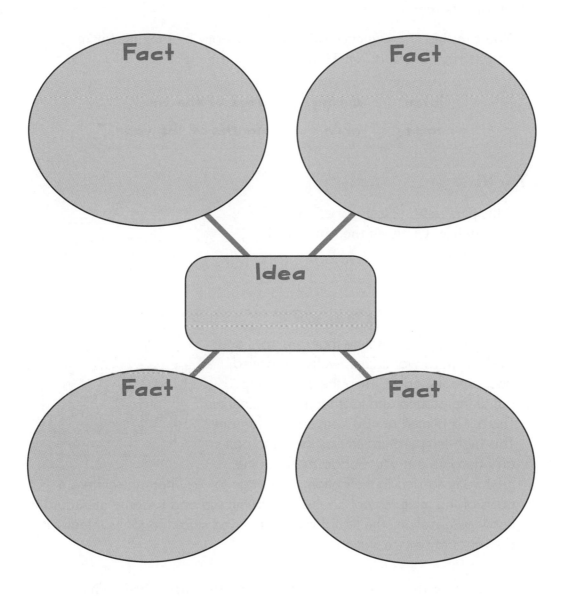

On Your Own

Now use another sheet of paper to write a paragraph about your idea. Use the facts from your idea web.

2

What Is Sequence?

Sequence means time order, or 1-2-3 order. If several things happen in a story, they happen in a sequence. One event happens first, and it is followed by another event.

You can find the sequence of events in a story by looking for time words, such as *first*, *next*, and *last*. Here is a list of time words:

later	during	days of the week
today	while	months of the year

Try It!

This paragraph tells a story. Try to follow the sequence. Circle all the time words.

Making Gasoline

Producing the gasoline that runs cars and trucks is hard work. First, wells are drilled deep into the earth. Then the oil is pumped out of the ground and taken to large refineries. There it is heated to 400°C in special furnaces. This high temperature causes the oil to boil and become a mixture of gases. Then the mixture is carried to the bottom of a large tower. There the different parts of the mixture cool on the way to the top and become the liquid we know as gasoline. The liquid is collected and stored in tanks. Finally it is delivered to service stations.

Try putting these events in the order that they happened. What happened first? Write the number **1** on the line by that sentence. Then write the number **2** by the sentence that tells what happened next. Write the number **3** by the sentence that tells what happened last.

_____ Oil is heated in furnaces.

_____ Gasoline is sent to service stations.

_____ Oil is pumped from the ground.

Practice with Sequence

Here are some practice sequence questions. The first two are already answered. You can do the third one on your own.

___A___ **1.** When is the oil pumped out of the ground?
  A. after the wells are drilled
  B. while it is heated
  C. after it is taken to the refineries

Look at the question. It has the words "oil pumped." Find those words in the story about gasoline. You will find the sentence, "Then the oil is pumped out of the ground and taken to large refineries." Find the time word in that sentence. The word is *then*. Look at the action just before that sentence. It says, "First, wells are drilled deep into the earth." The oil is pumped after the wells are drilled, so A is correct.

___C___ **2.** What happens just before the oil becomes a mixture of gases?
  A. The oil is heated.
  B. The mixture cools.
  C. The oil boils.

Look at the question carefully. Notice the time word *before*. Notice also that the word *just* is there. The question is asking what happens *just before* the oil becomes a mixture of gases. In the story you will find this sentence: "This high temperature causes the oil to boil and become a mixture of gases." Answer C is correct. Answers A and B are not correct because they tell what happens before and after the oil begins to boil.

_____ **3.** What happens after the oil is stored in tanks?
  A. It is collected.
  B. It is delivered.
  C. It is boiled.

Read each story. After each story you will answer questions about the sequence of events in the story. Remember, sequence is the order of things.

A Meal of Eel?

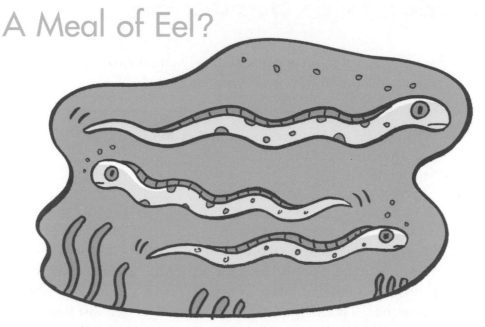

The eel is a fish, but it has no scales. It is able to breathe in or out of the water. It looks like a snake. The American eel can live in both salt water and freshwater. American eels begin life as eggs in the sea near Puerto Rico. When they hatch from eggs, the babies look like thin, see-through leaves. For about a year, they drift on ocean currents and eat plankton. Plankton is the tiny animal and plant life in water.

Eventually, currents carry the eels thousand of miles north to the United States. There the young eels swim to bodies of freshwater, such as lakes and rivers, and feed on the fish and animals at the bottom. The eels are strong, and some of them can even climb up waterfalls and dams.

As the eels grow older, their bodies become longer and turn yellow. It takes about 10 years for these yellow eels to become full-grown. When they become adults, they change color again! They turn black and silver, and then they are called silver eels. Females grow from 3 to 4 feet long, while males reach about 1 $1/2$ feet in length.

Finally it's time to make eggs, so they all swim to reach the ocean. Sometimes they may slither across land through wet grass. Then the silver eels make the long trip back to the Sargasso Sea near Puerto Rico. There, the cycle starts over.

Some people eat eels. In Europe and Asia, eels are considered to be a special dish. In America, some restaurants serve grilled eel. Have you had eel? You can eat them with barbecue sauce!

1. Put these events in the order that they happened. What happened first? Write the number **1** on the line by that sentence. Then write the number **2** by the sentence that tells what happened next. Write the number **3** by the sentence that tells what happened last.

_____ Yellow eels mature to be silver eels.

_____ Silver eels swim back to the Sargasso Sea.

_____ Currents carry baby eels to the United States.

_____ **2.** When do eels eat plankton?
    A. before they've hatched
    B. while they drift in the ocean
    C. after they eat fish

_____ **3.** When do the eels swim in fresh water?
    A. before they look like leaves
    B. after they reach the United States
    C. after they lay eggs

_____ **4.** When do the yellow eels turn black and silver?
    A. after they make eggs
    B. when they become adults
    C. before they are see-through

_____ **5.** When do eels return to the Sargasso Sea?
    A. when they swim up dams
    B. when they are ready to breathe air
    C. when it's time to make eggs

On September 30, 1492, sailors on three ships, the *Pinta*, the *Niña*, and the *Santa Maria*, were worried. They had left the shores of Spain weeks before. No one knew what lay ahead. They hoped for a safe voyage across the vast ocean. They also hoped that they would see land soon, but land was nowhere in sight.

Then their luck changed. They began to notice signs of land. First they saw a large flock of birds flying overhead. They even heard the birds call out. Then the crew of the *Pinta* spotted green reeds floating in the water.

Sailors on the other ships also began to see signs of land. Those on the *Niña* saw a stick covered with barnacles. Barnacles are shellfish that grow on rocks and the bottoms of boats. The sailors began to have more hope.

Christopher Columbus was the leader of the group. He urged the crew to be more watchful than ever. He asked that they fire a cannon when they spotted land.

Then at ten o'clock at night on October 11, Columbus saw a light. Columbus did not trust his own senses. He knew his strong desire to reach land might be causing his imagination to run wild. He asked two other men if they saw the light. The first man claimed to see the light, but the second one did not.

The Moon rose before midnight and lit the water. With their eyes scanning the water, the sailors on all three ships watched silently. Two hours later everyone heard the blast of a cannon. The men on the *Pinta* had seen land. All the men cheered.

1. Put these events in the order that they happened. What happened first? Write the number **1** on the line by that sentence. Then write the number **2** by the sentence that tells what happened next. Write the number **3** by the sentence that tells what happened last.

_____ The sailors saw signs of land.

_____ The sailors heard the blast of a cannon.

_____ The sailors cheered.

_____ **2.** When did the sailors notice signs of land?
  A. before they left Spain
  B. before October 11
  C. after they heard a cannon blast

_____ **3.** When did sailors see reeds in the water?
  A. after a whale swam by
  B. after birds flew by
  C. after everyone cheered

_____ **4.** When did Columbus see a light?
  A. at ten o'clock at night
  B. at midnight
  C. at dawn

_____ **5.** When did everyone hear the sound of the cannon blast?
  A. before Columbus saw land
  B. before the *Pinta* sank
  C. after the *Pinta* crew saw land

For more than 160 million years, dinosaurs ruled Earth. Some were no larger than chickens. Others were more than 100 feet long and may have weighed 100 tons. Some dinosaurs ate plants. Others ate other dinosaurs! The last of these reptiles vanished about 65 million years ago.

Until recently scientists have thought that dinosaurs disappeared slowly. They thought that the temperature on Earth cooled. Plants and dinosaurs that were used to warm weather couldn't survive the cold climate. Also, early mammals might have eaten dinosaur eggs. Over many years, all the dinosaurs finally died.

In 1980, two scientists came up with a new idea about how the dinosaurs vanished. Luis Alvarez and his son Walter studied a layer of clay. In this clay the two men found iridium. This substance is rarely found in Earth's crust. It is found in meteors that fall to Earth from outer space. The two men now think that dinosaurs might have died quickly.

The Alvarezes think that millions of years ago a huge meteorite might have slammed into warm, sunny Earth. The impact sent a huge cloud of dust into the air. For months the dust cloud shut out the light of the Sun. With no sunlight all plants on Earth died. The plant-eating dinosaurs had no food, so they died too. The meat-eating dinosaurs then died quickly, because their food source was gone.

Today not all scientists agree with the idea of "quick death." Some think the idea should be studied. As time goes by, scientists will continue to study how the dinosaurs disappeared.

1. Put these events in the order that they happened. What happened first? Write the number **1** on the line by that sentence. Then write the number **2** by the sentence that tells what happened next. Write the number **3** by the sentence that tells what happened last.

_____ The Alvarezes found iridium.

_____ The Alvarezes developed a new idea.

_____ The Alvarezes studied the clay.

_____ **2.** When did dinosaurs vanish from Earth?
    A. about 65 million years ago
    B. more than 100 million years ago
    C. before a meteorite landed

_____ **3.** What happened as Earth grew colder?
    A. The mammals disappeared.
    B. The dinosaurs died.
    C. Meteorites fell.

_____ **4.** When did the huge dust cloud fill the air?
    A. after the plants died
    B. when the meteorite fell
    C. after the dinosaurs died

_____ **5.** According to the Alvarezes, when did the dinosaurs die?
    A. while Earth was sunny
    B. thousands of years ago
    C. after sunlight was shut out

Message in the Sky

Skywriting began in England during World War I. The Royal Air Force made signals with smoke from airplanes. The signals could be seen from great distances. In 1922, the first words written in the sky over America were "Hello USA." That year skywriting began to be used for advertising. It stayed popular until the 1950s when more ads began appearing on television.

Here's how one pilot makes letters ¼ mile tall. First he writes the letters backward on a piece of paper and tapes that in his plane. Next he walks through turns and loops he'll have to fly. Then, in a plane that used to be a crop duster, he takes off and rises about 9,000 feet. He locates landmarks on the ground that will help him keep his lines straight. At last he flips a switch and smoke blasts out of the exhaust pipes.

It's challenging to put a message in the sky. The pilot counts seconds to know when to turn the smoke on and off. He has to concentrate to write backward, especially the numbers *2* and *5*. Wind moves the letters, so the pilot watches their shadows on the ground or their pattern in the sky. If it's a snowy day, the pilot in the plane won't see the white letters over the white land, but observers on the ground will see them in the sky. The view is awesome.

1. Put these events in the order that they happened. What happened first? Write the number **1** on the line by that sentence. Then write the number **2** by the sentence that tells what happened next. Write the number **3** by the sentence that tells what happened last.

_____ The television was used more for advertising.

_____ Skywriting was used to send signals in the war.

_____ Skywriting was used for advertising.

_____ **2.** When did skywriting begin?
   A. during World War I
   B. during the 1950s
   C. during the Great Depression

_____ **3.** When does the pilot walk through the turns and loops he will fly?
   A. after he writes the letters on paper
   B. after he rises to 9,000 feet
   C. after he releases smoke from the plane

_____ **4.** When does the pilot write letters in the sky?
   A. before takeoff
   B. after he jumps from a plane
   C. after he locates landmarks

_____ **5.** When are letters in the sky invisible to the pilot?
   A. when the pilot lands
   B. when the Sun is out
   C. when snow covers the ground

Ready! Get Set! Pedal!

Some people put their bicycles away once they learn how to drive a car. For many people, bicycling is not just an easy way of getting around town. It is also an exciting sport. Serious cyclists often enter races.

One kind of race is the time trial. Each racer leaves the starting line at a different time and pedals hard toward the finish line. The cyclist who covers the distance in the shortest amount of time wins the race. A time trial is a safe race for beginners because the bicycles are spread out and are not as likely to run into each other.

Another kind of race is more difficult. A few city blocks are closed to traffic. Then all the racers line up in a tight pack and begin racing at the same time. They cover many laps, going around and around the city blocks. The race requires more than speed. It also requires skillful handling of the bicycle as it darts around other bicycles. The racer who completes all the laps first is the winner.

Road races are usually the longest cycling contests. Racers have to cover anywhere from 35 miles to almost 3,000 miles. The race course may be a straight stretch of road or a long series of roads across the country. The prize goes to the first person who crosses the finish line.

Between races cyclists stay in condition by doing exercises that build their strength so they can keep riding for long periods of time. Some cyclists ride on a special raceway called a velodrome. It's a safe place to practice because there is no automobile traffic.

As cyclists become more experienced, they often join bicycling groups and become licensed racers. Then they can enter special races all over the country. Coaches watch the cyclists in these special races. The coaches are always looking for winners to join national teams. If you're a cyclist, keep pedaling! You could become a star!

1. Put these events in the order that they happened. What happened first? Write the number **1** on the line by that sentence. Then write the number **2** by the sentence that tells what happened next. Write the number **3** by the sentence that tells what happened last.

_____ The cyclists cover many laps.

_____ The winner crosses the finish line.

_____ The racers wait at the starting line.

_____ **2.** When does a cyclist finish the time trial?
   A. after the racer has covered the distance
   B. before the cyclist begins racing
   C. when the racer goes around the city blocks

_____ **3.** When do some cyclists build their strength?
   A. in between races
   B. right before a race is over
   C. during a race

_____ **4.** What happens after cyclists become more experienced?
   A. They enter time trials.
   B. They ride around town.
   C. They often become licensed racers.

_____ **5.** When do coaches of national teams watch cyclists?
   A. after a cyclist enters special races
   B. before a racer enters time trials
   C. during regular road races

Umbrellas

Umbrellas are useful, rain or shine. They have been used for both kinds of weather for more than 3,000 years. You might say that umbrellas are dripping with history.

Early Egyptian rulers used them in ceremonies. Leaders of old Japan walked under red umbrellas. They were a sign of power. The kings of Burma rode on white elephants under white umbrellas. People in Greece and Rome also used umbrellas long ago. The umbrellas of early times were used in warm lands as protection against the Sun.

By the 1600s umbrellas had appeared in northern Europe. In these countries they were used on rainy days, too. The umbrellas were thought to be big and clumsy. They were used only by people who didn't have carriages.

By the 1700s umbrellas had become more popular in countries such as England. During this time many umbrellas had jewels and fancy handles made of rare wood. Some umbrellas had hollow handles. Perfume, knives, and even pens and paper were kept in these handles.

Umbrellas were improved in the 1800s. Before that time most were made with whalebone spokes. They weighed 10 pounds! By 1826, their weight was down to 1 1/2 pounds. Steel frames were first used in 1852. Covers for these umbrellas were made of waxed silk or oiled paper.

Today's umbrellas are very light. Some people think they turn inside out too easily, but modern umbrellas do have some good points. For example, they fold up into smaller packages. Some have plastic windows in them so people can see where they're walking. When the rain comes down, people can pop open their umbrellas quickly and be on their way.

1. Put these events in the order that they happened. What happened first? Write the number **1** on the line by that sentence. Then write the number **2** by the sentence that tells what happened next. Write the number **3** by the sentence that tells what happened last.

_____ Umbrellas weighed 10 pounds.

_____ Umbrellas folded up into smaller packages.

_____ Umbrellas weighed 1 ½ pounds.

_____ **2.** When were umbrellas used mainly to protect against the sun?
   A. before the 1600s
   B. by the 1700s
   C. during modern times

_____ **3.** When were umbrellas first used in northern Europe?
   A. before the 1500s
   B. during the 600s
   C. by the 1600s

_____ **4.** When were umbrellas used to protect against rain?
   A. before they were used in Burma
   B. during early times in Egypt
   C. after they appeared in northern Europe

_____ **5.** When were umbrellas decorated with jewels?
   A. before they first appeared in northern Europe
   B. when they were first used in Greece and Rome
   C. after they had become more popular in England

Toy on a String

Long ago in the jungles of the Philippine Islands, soldiers developed a powerful weapon. They took heavy stones and carved a ridge around the outside of each one. Next they wrapped a thick rope about 20 feet long around the ridge. The stone could be thrown out quickly with tremendous force and then pulled back. Enemies had a hard time fighting these weapons. The Filipino soldiers named them *yo-yos*, a word that means "to return."

In the early 1900s, a man named Pedro Flores made a toy out of the yo-yo. He carved small yo-yos out of wood and put strings around them. Then he gave them to children. The toys could be moved up and down by handling the string just right. When Flores moved to California in the 1920s, he started his own yo-yo factory. Children loved yo-yos, and so did many adults.

Then Donald F. Duncan saw the yo-yos. He thought he could make them even more popular all across the country. He bought Flores's company. Then he developed a stronger string, which he called a slip-string. The slip-string helped children perform all sorts of tricks with a yo-yo. To help sell the toy, Duncan sent yo-yo experts all over the United States. These experts taught the tricks to children and their parents.

Playing with yo-yos soon became a national sport. For a while the Duncan factory in Luck, Wisconsin, was turning out 3,600 yo-yos per hour. Luck was called the "Yo-Yo Capital of the World." During World War II, yo-yo production slowed. Materials were hard to get during that time.

After the war the yo-yo business picked up again. Plastic yo-yos were developed. They lasted longer, and it was easier to do tricks with them. In one yo-yo contest, a man named John Winslow won a special prize. He played with a yo-yo for 120 hours without stopping.

1. Put these events in the order that they happened. What happened first? Write the number **1** on the line by that sentence. Then write the number **2** by the sentence that tells what happened next. Write the number **3** by the sentence that tells what happened last.

_____ Flores moved to California.

_____ Soldiers developed yo-yos.

_____ Flores carved yo-yos out of wood.

_____ **2.** When were yo-yos first made as toys?
   A. in the early 1900s
   B. 20 years ago
   C. after Flores moved to California

_____ **3.** When were yo-yos first given to children?
   A. after experts taught them
   B. when yo-yos were made of plastic
   C. after Flores made wooden yo-yos

_____ **4.** When was material for yo-yos hard to find?
   A. before 1920
   B. when Filipinos used yo-yos as weapons
   C. during World War II

_____ **5.** What happened after plastic yo-yos were developed?
   A. Nobody liked them.
   B. A man won a special prize.
   C. Each hour 3,600 were made.

Windsurfing

Have you ever seen someone glide across a lake on what looks like a surfboard with a sail? That's a windsurfer.

Windsurfers use a sailboard. It is a board much like a surfboard. It is made of plastic or fiberglass. A mast, or vertical pole, stands in the center of the board. The sail is hooked to the mast. There is a plastic window in the sail so that the surfer can see where the board is going. The surfer keeps his or her balance and steers by holding onto a boom. The boom is a horizontal bar that is attached to the sail. The surfer lifts the sail out of the water with a rope that is attached to the boom.

There have been many arguments over who first invented the sailboard. In 1982, a court ruled that a 12-year-old British boy had made the first sailboard in 1958. This sport first became popular in Europe in the 1970s.

In 1968 two Americans, Jim Drake and Hoyle Schweitzer, designed a flat-bottomed sailboard. It became very popular. It is easiest to learn how to windsurf on flat-bottomed sailboards. Learning this sport is not hard, but it takes practice. First you must be able to stand on the sailboard and pull the sail up out of the water. This takes a great amount of strength and balance. Then you must learn how to turn the sail to make the best use of the wind.

Funboarding is a special kind of windsurfing. Funboards were designed to be used in strong winds. In 1977, Larry Stanley added footstraps to a funboard. This let surfers ride big waves and jump out of the water with their boards. Funboarding is a popular sport in Hawaii.

1. Put these events in the order that they happened. What happened first? Write the number **1** on the line by that sentence. Then write the number **2** by the sentence that tells what happened next. Write the number **3** by the sentence that tells what happened last.

_____ Footstraps were added to funboards.

_____ Drake and Schweitzer designed a board with a flat bottom.

_____ A court decided who had invented the sailboard.

_____ **2.** When was the sailboard invented?
- **A.** during 1958
- **B.** after 1982
- **C.** during the 1984 Olympics

_____ **3.** When did windsurfing first become popular?
- **A.** before World War II
- **B.** during the 1970s
- **C.** at the same time that surfing became popular

_____ **4.** When do you pull the sail out of the water?
- **A.** while you are sailing
- **B.** before you turn the sail in the wind
- **C.** after you learn to ride big ocean waves

_____ **5.** When were footstraps added to funboards?
- **A.** just before strong winds rose
- **B.** after the 1982 trial
- **C.** during 1977

Writing Roundup

Read the paragraph below. Think about the sequence, or time order.
Answer the questions in complete sentences.

Janet places bands on baby bald eagles' legs to help study the birds. First Janet straps spurs onto her shoes and loops a rope around a tree. Next she climbs up to the eagles' nest and ties herself to the tree. Then she slowly pulls a baby close with her hooked stick. The babies can't fly, but they might jump from the nest if frightened. Finally Janet attaches a metal band to each bird's leg.

1. What is the first thing Janet does?

_____

_____

2. When does Janet tie herself to the tree?

_____

_____

3. When does Janet clamp the band on one of the eagle's legs?

_____

_____

4. When might a baby jump from the nest?

_____

_____

Prewriting

Think about something that you have done, such as doing your laundry, training to improve your fitness, or tie-dyeing a T-shirt. Write the events in sequence below.

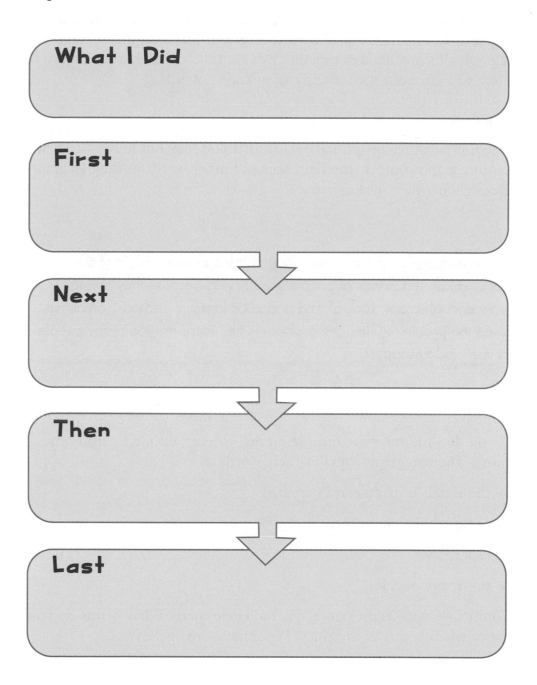

What I Did

First

Next

Then

Last

On Your Own

Now use another sheet of paper to write a paragraph about what you have done. Write the events in the order that they happened. Use time order words.

What Is Context?

Context means all the words in a sentence or all the sentences in a paragraph. In a sentence all the words together make up the context. In a paragraph all the sentences together make up the context. You can use the context to figure out the meaning of unknown words.

Try It!

The following paragraph has a word that you may not know. See whether you can use the context (the sentences and other words in the paragraph) to decide what the word means.

Scientists are very concerned about **famine** in many parts of the world today. Thousands of people are starving because they cannot grow enough crops. Lack of rain and poor farming methods sometimes cause the problem. Often the problem is that there are too many people for the land to support.

If you don't know what **famine** means, you can decide by using the context. The paragraph contains these words:

Clue: thousands of people are starving

Clue: cannot grow enough crops

Clue: lack of rain

Clue: too many people

Find these clues in the paragraph and circle them. What words do you think of when you read the clues? Write the words below:

_____

Did you write *hunger* or a similar word? The context clue words tell you that **famine** is a lack of food.

Working with Context

This unit asks questions that you can answer by using context clues in paragraphs. There are two kinds of paragraphs. The paragraphs in the first part of this unit have blank spaces in them. You can use the context clues in the paragraphs to decide which words should go in each space. Here is an example:

Baboons live in groups. Usually there are about 60 __1__ in the group, but there may be as many as 200 or as few as 10. Living in a tribe __2__ the baboons from their enemies.

__C__ 1. **A.** jars   **B.** museums   **C.** individuals   **D.** patients

_____ 2. **A.** hides   **B.** safeguards   **C.** leads   **D.** grazes

Look at the answer choices for question 1. Try putting each choice in the paragraph to see which one makes the most sense. Treat the paragraph as a puzzle. Determine which pieces don't fit and which piece fits best. The paragraph tells about baboons living in groups. It doesn't make sense to say that there are 60 *jars*, *museums*, or *patients*. *Individuals* (answer **C**) is the only choice that makes sense in this paragraph. Now try to answer question 2 on your own.

The paragraphs in the second part of this unit are different. For these you figure out the meaning of a word that is printed in **dark letters** in the paragraph. Here is an example:

Many vines have long **clusters** of sweet-smelling flowers. Vines will climb posts and other objects. They are often planted for their beauty and shade.

In this paragraph, the word in dark type is **clusters**. Find the context clues, and treat the paragraph as a puzzle. Then choose a word that means the same as **clusters**.

_____ **3.** In this paragraph, the word **clusters** means
     A. animals   **C.** drinks
     B. stems   **D.** bunches

Read the passages and answer the questions about context. Remember, context is a way to learn new words by thinking about the other words used in a story.

Saudi Arabia is a desert country where ___1___ is always a problem. Some years ago the king planned to tow a huge ___2___ from the South Pole to supply his country with water.

_____ 1. A. chocolate   B. drought   C. camel   D. fashion

_____ 2. A. fish   B. fountain   C. leaf   D. iceberg

More than 100 years ago, Charles Babbage drew a ___3___ for a machine that could calculate. If built, the ___4___ would have been the first computer.

_____ 3. A. diagram   B. bet   C. cake   D. problem

_____ 4. A. water   B. device   C. book   D. game

Watching television can be ___5___. After a while, you may feel bored. That's the time to come up with your own ___6___. Make a new friend, start a hobby, or learn a skill.

_____ 5. A. general   B. housework   C. usual   D. relaxing

_____ 6. A. elevator   B. sunshine   C. recreation   D. recipes

Some lawmakers think there should be laws about false teeth. They want these ___7___ teeth to have a special ___8___ to identify the owner in case of accident.

_____ 7. A. clean   B. sharp   C. open   D. artificial

_____ 8. A. numeral   B. river   C. tooth   D. brush

In ancient times ____9____ in different parts of the world named the stars. In almost every ____10____, stars were named for animals.

_____ 9. **A.** seas   **B.** astronomers   **C.** stars   **D.** meters

_____10. **A.** student   **B.** civilization   **C.** third   **D.** time

---

The first movie with a ____11____ about traveling to the Moon was made in 1902 in France. In the film, moon walkers put up umbrellas to avoid the ____12____ of the Sun.

_____11. **A.** check   **B.** camera   **C.** producer   **D.** plot

_____12. **A.** hobbies   **B.** rain   **C.** movie   **D.** rays

---

The continents are slowly drifting apart. Since they are not ____13____, North and South America will one day ____14____ entirely. Then the ocean will flow between them.

_____13. **A.** clean   **B.** stationary   **C.** moving   **D.** land

_____14. **A.** name   **B.** reverse   **C.** separate   **D.** lock

---

Deer know each other from the scent on the ____15____ of their hind legs. Each deer has a different scent. A ____16____ knows its mother by sniffing her hind legs.

_____15. **A.** shoes   **B.** trim   **C.** ankles   **D.** head

_____16. **A.** monkey   **B.** fawn   **C.** father   **D.** turn

The kangaroo and the wombat keep their newborns very close after birth. Many of them raise their young in their __1__ until the babies have __2__ strength to leave.

_____ 1. **A.** farm **B.** tree **C.** steady **D.** pouch

_____ 2. **A.** no **B.** sufficient **C.** many **D.** national

A man named Richebourg was a spy in France nearly 300 years ago. He was only 23 inches tall. He was most __3__ when he was disguised as an __4__ being carried by his nurse.

_____ 3. **A.** modern **B.** friendly **C.** successful **D.** French

_____ 4. **A.** infant **B.** extra **C.** armor **D.** owl

Many people have an __5__ of bats as bloodthirsty animals. This is not a true picture. Most bats live on a __6__ of insects, flowers, or fruit.

_____ 5. **A.** answer **B.** action **C.** elevator **D.** image

_____ 6. **A.** diet **B.** plate **C.** tree **D.** bush

Cheese factories __7__ many health inspections. Some people feel that the taste of cheese has gotten worse. It has been __8__ by processes designed to make it safe.

_____ 7. **A.** remind **B.** require
        C. read **D.** milk

_____ 8. **A.** altered **B.** helped
        C. freed **D.** risen

Many movies show deserts as hot areas covered with sand ___9___. In real life the typical desert does look ___10___, but it is covered with rocks, not sand.

_____ 9. **A.** lakes   **B.** castles   **C.** sneezes   **D.** dunes

_____10. **A.** watery   **B.** cool   **C.** harsh   **D.** carpeted

Laws about using water to ___11___ crops go back to ancient times. Thousands of years ago, the Babylonians had many laws and ___12___ for the use of water.

_____11. **A.** irrigate   **B.** burn   **C.** park   **D.** destroy

_____12. **A.** rulers   **B.** regulations   **C.** families   **D.** phones

The coconut got its name from the Portuguese word *coco*. This word describes the ___13___ on the face of someone who is in pain. The "face" of the coconut seems to have this same ___14___ look.

_____13. **A.** scars   **B.** expression   **C.** love   **D.** teeth

_____14. **A.** smiling   **B.** partly   **C.** miserable   **D.** watch

The fruit of the banana plant takes from three to five months to ___15___ completely. Bananas don't ripen ___16___ unless picked. This is why they are picked when they are still green.

_____15. **A.** talk   **B.** care   **C.** mature   **D.** cease

_____16. **A.** properly   **B.** tomorrow   **C.** bubbly   **D.** madly

William Enos did not have a driver's ____1____. He could not operate a car, but he invented stop signs and one-way streets. He also wrote the first ____2____ of traffic regulations.

_____ 1. **A.** job   **B.** speed   **C.** license   **D.** ticket

_____ 2. **A.** play   **B.** song   **C.** manual   **D.** street

---

One kind of caterpillar can ____3____ itself. It puffs up its head and part of its body into a triangle that looks like a snake's head. When it ____4____ a snake, it may scare away enemies.

_____ 3. **A.** wrap   **B.** feed   **C.** disguise   **D.** climb

_____ 4. **A.** mimics   **B.** sees   **C.** follows   **D.** chases

---

Rachel Jackson did not want her husband Andrew to be a ____5____ for president. She ____6____ his decision to run for office, but she did not try to stop him.

_____ 5. **A.** candidate   **B.** senator   **C.** voter   **D.** failure

_____ 6. **A.** liked   **B.** regretted   **C.** halted   **D.** wished

---

Ida Lewis, a light keeper's daughter, kept the light burning in the lighthouse at Lime Rock Light in Rhode Island. She was only 15 when she rescued four men from the sea. Their boat had ____7____. This ____8____ and others like it made her famous. She is credited with saving lives.

_____ 7. **A.** sailed
         B. won
         C. capsized
         D. floated

_____ 8. **A.** woman
         B. light
         C. fiction
         D. incident

The bagpipe is a musical instrument played in Scotland. It makes a lonely, __9__ sound. One pipe plays the melody while the other three play low __10__ notes.

_____ **9. A.** moist   **B.** angry   **C.** forlorn   **D.** misty

_____ **10. A.** sick   **B.** narrow   **C.** argue   **D.** bass

---

In 1908, the president of an automobile company put on an exciting demonstration. He __11__ the parts of three different cars. Then the cars were put back together. This showed that cars could be built with parts that were interchangeable. __12__ each part could fit only the car it was made for.

_____ **11. A.** melted   **B.** jumbled   **C.** waited   **D.** froze

_____ **12. A.** Previously   **B.** Above   **C.** Beneath   **D.** Beside

---

In the Middle Ages, a __13__ did more than just cut hair. This person would often act as a doctor and perform __14__ on sick people.

_____ **13. A.** man   **B.** writer   **C.** barber   **D.** wife

_____ **14. A.** operations   **B.** jokes   **C.** weddings   **D.** lights

---

People who can't use their arms or legs the way most others do are called __15__. They learn to do things new ways. Adults who can't use their leg muscles might learn to drive a car using hand switches. Some people may learn how to cook while standing with __16__.

_____ **15. A.** tired   **B.** disabled   **C.** young   **D.** sir

_____ **16. A.** tables   **B.** elevators   **C.** curbs   **D.** crutches

A sightseeing ___1___ of London always includes a look at Big Ben. Big Ben is neither a clock nor the tower that holds it. It is the bell that ___2___ every hour.

_____ 1. A. shape   B. dog
        C. tour   D. lake

_____ 2. A. breaks   B. chimes
        C. cracks   D. asks

Some Americans are ___3___ of the difference between England and Great Britain. It's a mistake to think that they are the same. England is only one part of the island of Great Britain. Great Britain is the large island that ___4___ England, Wales, and Scotland.

_____ 3. A. upset   B. wild   C. ignorant   D. sad

_____ 4. A. leaves   B. includes   C. draws   D. centers

The Chinese and English languages do not have ___5___ rules. In Chinese, for example, verbs do not have tenses, and there is no way to tell whether a noun is singular or ___6___, except from context.

_____ 5. A. cheerful   B. later   C. chemical   D. similar

_____ 6. A. adjective   B. alone   C. plural   D. lazy

Camels are known for their ___7___ to go for days and even weeks without water. This is not because camels use their humps for water ___8___. The humps are all fat.

_____ 7. A. capacity
        B. friends
        C. failing
        D. humor

_____ 8. A. sports
        B. strainers
        C. storage
        D. faucets

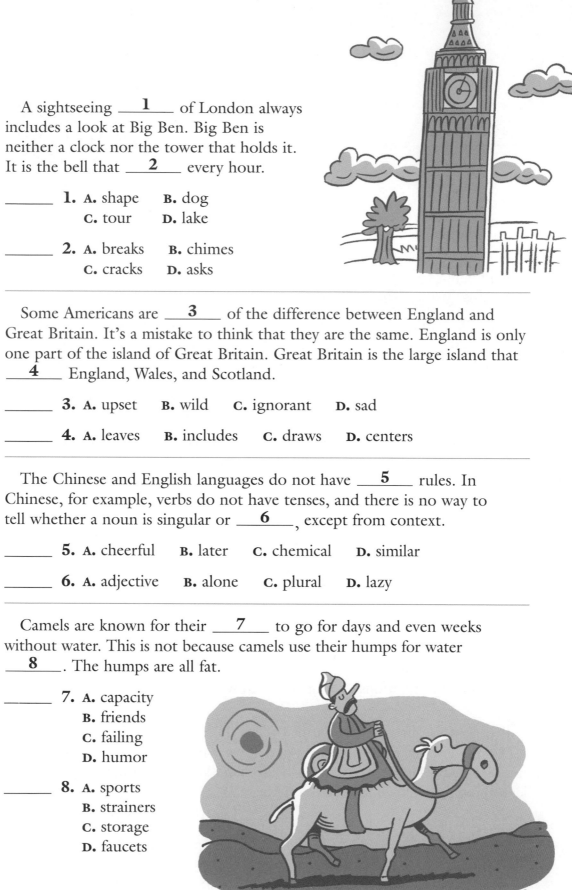

The deepest ___9___ in the United States is not the Grand Canyon. It is Hells Canyon. The ___10___ at Hells Canyon is greater than the one at the Grand Canyon by half a mile.

_____ 9. A. water   B. pond   C. thinker   D. gorge

_____10. A. flyer   B. animal   C. chasm   D. hill

A small, seaside ___11___ had a terrible problem. It had too many ___12___. These bloodsucking insects bit the tourists. The town solved its problem. It brought in hundreds of dragonflies, which feed on the pests.

_____11. A. community   B. boat   C. anchor   D. tree

_____12. A. frogs   B. mosquitoes   C. woodpeckers   D. things

Peter Stuyvesant was one of the most disliked governors in the New World, but he also began the first American fire ___13___ system. He had people ___14___ chimneys for possible fire dangers.

_____13. A. prevention   B. starting   C. average   D. inning

_____14. A. launch   B. welcome   C. inspect   D. punch

Helicopters are lifted into the air by one or two ___15___ wings. These fast-turning wings whirl through the air. They work against gravity to produce lift. Lift keeps the helicopter ___16___.

_____15. A. rotating   B. slow   C. serious   D. fixed

_____16. A. engine   B. heavy   C. pilot   D. aloft

The king cobra is a very dangerous snake. Its bite can kill an elephant in three hours. Most animals attack only when threatened, but the king cobra will attack without being **provoked**.

_____ **1.** In this paragraph, the word **provoked** means
    A. rescued   **C.** affected
    B. given a reason   **D.** poisoned

The tall buildings called skyscrapers might not have been built without the Chicago Fire of 1871. The fire **devastated** the wooden buildings of the city. The first skyscraper was built on the ruins of the fire.

_____ **2.** In this paragraph, the word **devastated** means
    A. built   **C.** destroyed
    B. designed   **D.** sold

Scientists have wondered how the Moon came to be. More and more facts **reinforce** the idea that the Moon was probably created by a tremendous crash. A planet the size of Mars hit Earth, and the Moon broke off from Earth.

_____ **3.** In this paragraph, the word **reinforce** means
    A. plan   **C.** trim
    B. send   **D.** support

On the ocean, distance is measured in **nautical** miles. This kind of mile is about 800 feet longer than the mile used for measuring land.

_____ **4.** In this paragraph, the word **nautical** means
    A. sea   **C.** shorter
    B. whale   **D.** probably untrue

How would you like a soup made from a bird's nest? Diners in China **consider** bird's nest soup delicious. The right kind of bird's nests for this soup are found in caves.

_____ **5.** In this paragraph, the word **consider** means
  A. make   **C.** take
  B. think   **D.** sell

Roberto Clemente was the first Hispanic player to be admitted into the Baseball Hall of Fame. He won many awards for his **superb** hitting and fielding skills.

_____ **6.** In this paragraph, the word **superb** means
  A. poor   **C.** outstanding
  B. quick   **D.** outdoor

The Trail of Tears was a journey that took place in the United States. White settlers wanted the land where some Native Americans lived. The government forced these native people to move away from their homes. Thousands of them died on the **tragic** trip.

_____ **7.** In this paragraph, the word **tragic** means
  A. sad   **C.** rude
  B. happy   **D.** brief

Many things we use every day were **invented** in the 1800s. Someone from England gave us the bicycle. An American designed the safety pin.

_____ **8.** In this paragraph, the
    word **invented** means
      A. first made
      B. finally broken
      C. fixed
      D. always needed

Divers uncover many **underwater** secrets. Ancient ships, old cities, and works of art have been found. The sea has hidden some of its treasures for thousands of years.

_____ **1.** In this paragraph, the word **underwater** means

    A. on a mountain   **C.** near

    B. in the sea   **D.** blue

Yellowstone is the oldest national park in the United States. Congress **established** it as a national park in 1872.

_____ **2.** In this paragraph, the word **established** means

    A. cut   **C.** loved

    B. crowded   **D.** started

Some batters think that a curve ball drops 5 feet from home plate. Some have the **view** that it falls 10 feet. Some say that a certain star pitcher's curve ball looked as if it were rolling off a table.

_____ **3.** In this paragraph, the word **view** means

    A. bat   **C.** fly

    B. opinion   **D.** eyes

Popcorn is different from other kinds of corn. The **kernels** have hard shells. The water inside each piece of corn turns to steam. The steam makes the pieces of corn swell and pop.

_____ **4.** In this paragraph, the word **kernels** means

    A. soldiers

    B. cobs

    C. flavors

    D. seeds

The mummies of Egypt are very old, so people assume the Egyptians had special ways of **embalming**. Actually it was the dry air that helped preserve their dead.

_____ **5.** In this paragraph, the word **embalming** means

     A. making pyramids   **C.** keeping things alive

     B. preventing decay   **D.** dealing with heat

Modern **appliances** make our lives much easier. Washing machines, dryers, and dishwashers make completing household chores much faster than in the old days. The "good old days" meant hard work!

_____ **6.** In this paragraph, the word **appliances** means

     A. movies   **C.** machines

     B. people   **D.** apples

Lincoln's **proclamation** ending slavery had no immediate effect. His announcement was made in the middle of the Civil War. The South ignored the order.

_____ **7.** In this paragraph, the word **proclamation** means

     A. secret message   **C.** review of the war

     B. official, public order   **D.** loud voice

Across deserts and mountains, Pony Express riders on horseback carried the mail in the Old West. Most riders were young boys. They needed great courage and skill. **Incompetent** riders couldn't do the job!

_____ **8.** In this paragraph, the word **incompetent** means

     A. genuine   **C.** independent

     B. poorly skilled   **D.** experienced

Lions are not as **noble** as people think. For instance, lions sometimes kill for no reason. They do not kill only to get food.

_____ **1.** In this paragraph, the word **noble** means
    A. strong   **C.** good
    B. mean   **D.** fierce

Some people think that W. C. Fields's **epitaph** reads: "I would rather be in Philadelphia." This is not true. The funny actor's tombstone says: "W. C. Fields, 1880–1946."

_____ **2.** In this paragraph, the word **epitaph** means
    A. dying words   **C.** most famous joke
    B. last telegram   **D.** words on a grave marker

A farmer can't build a new barn alone. To get help, farmers in the 1800s held barn raisings. The neighbors would **congregate** and work all day to complete the barn.

_____ **3.** In this paragraph, the word **congregate** means
    A. complain   **C.** come together
    B. work alone   **D.** leave

The Constitution does not say that a jury's **verdict** has to be agreed upon by all members. The idea of a jury trial is older than United States laws. It came to the United States from England.

_____ **4.** In this paragraph, the word **verdict** means
    A. dinner   **C.** invitation
    B. chamber   **D.** decision

At first the meaning of the word *nice* wasn't nice at all. *Nice* once meant "ignorant." It began to **imply** a more pleasant meaning after the sixteenth century.

_____ **5.** In this paragraph, the word **imply** means
    A. reply   **C.** understand
    B. suggest   **D.** remove

Many people believe that Rome is the oldest **metropolis** in use, but other cities are much older. Rome was founded in 753 B.C. Damascus, Syria, was founded in 3000 B.C.

_____ **6.** In this paragraph, the word **metropolis** means
    A. ruins   **C.** river
    B. government   **D.** city

The killer whale deserves its name in the wild. There it destroys dolphins, birds, and fish. However, a captured killer whale is **meek** and friendly to people.

_____ **7.** In this paragraph, the word **meek** means
    A. necessary   **C.** quietly obedient
    B. mean   **D.** easily discouraged

The opossum **utilizes** its tail for grasping. But baby opossums do not use their tails to hold onto the mother while riding on her back. They use their paws.

_____ **8.** In this paragraph, the word **utilizes** means
    A. uses   **C.** exercises
    B. holds   **D.** stretches

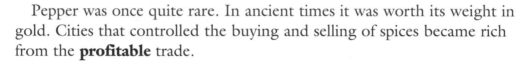

There's a house in Massachusetts **fashioned** entirely from newspapers. The walls and roof are pages glued together to form thick boards. The curtains are woven from the funny pages.

_____ **1.** In this paragraph, the word **fashioned** means

A. printed   **C.** read

B. built   **D.** clothed

Pepper was once quite rare. In ancient times it was worth its weight in gold. Cities that controlled the buying and selling of spices became rich from the **profitable** trade.

_____ **2.** In this paragraph, the word **profitable** means

A. cheap   **C.** well-paying

B. slow   **D.** confusing

In 1980, someone threw a grape more than 300 feet. A man caught the grape in his mouth. The **site** of this event was a football field in Louisiana.

_____ **3.** In this paragraph, the word **site** means

A. toss   **C.** time

B. place   **D.** game

In 1902, a man asked a woman to marry him. She said yes. They decided to wait a few years before they got married. They finally got around to **matrimony** in 1969.

_____ **4.** In this paragraph, the word **matrimony** means

A. talking   **C.** marrying

B. trying   **D.** dying

Animals that live in the desert are well protected. Their small bodies help them escape the heat that **scorches** the ground. Some animals stay in tunnels when the hot sun beats down.

_____ **5.** In this paragraph, the word **scorches** means
- **A.** buries
- **B.** waters
- **C.** burns
- **D.** digs

A woman in Australia and a woman in England were pen pals. Their **correspondence** lasted 75 years.

_____ **6.** In this paragraph, the word **correspondence** means
- **A.** letter writing
- **B.** friends
- **C.** phone calls
- **D.** mailbox

At many beaches people enter contests for building castles from sand. Some of the castles are very **elaborate**. They have towers, windows, and even bridges.

_____ **7.** In this paragraph, the word **elaborate** means
- **A.** sandy
- **B.** short
- **C.** plain
- **D.** fancy

Spanish explorers took gold from the New World aboard their ships. They tried to carry it to Europe. However, many of the ships sank before they reached their **destination**. The old ships still lie beneath the sea. The treasure awaits inside them.

_____ **8.** In this paragraph, the word **destination** means
- **A.** silver
- **B.** goal
- **C.** surface
- **D.** mountain

Writing Roundup

Read each paragraph. Write a word that makes sense on each line.

What a terrible day Nick had! Because of a sore throat,

he had to stay at home and miss the **(1)** _____.

To make matters worse, he couldn't even eat his favorite food,

(2) _____.

I'm sure Mrs. Soliz is the friendliest person in the whole

(3) _____. Whenever new families move into

our apartment building, she's the first one to greet them.

She always makes them feel **(4)** _____.

Jill is a pilot. She loves to fly high above the

(5) _____. From the air, cars look as

tiny as **(6)** _____.

Read each paragraph. Write a sentence that makes sense on each line.

Eric lives on a wildlife preserve where animals roam freely.
Each day he wonders what wild animal might come into his
front yard. **(1)** _____

_____ .

One morning Eric looked out his window. What a sight!
(2) _____ .

Quickly he got his camera. **(3)** _____

_____ .

The citizens planned to celebrate the one hundredth
anniversary of Springfield. One committee discussed how
to decorate the city hall. **(4)** _____

_____ .

The program committee couldn't decide what type of program
to have. **(5)** _____

_____ .

Then the mayor, Ms. Carter, had a suggestion.
(6) _____ .

What Is a Main Idea?

The main idea sentence of a paragraph tells what the paragraph is about. The other sentences are details or small parts. They add up to the main idea. The main idea sentence is often the first or last sentence in a paragraph, but you may find it in the middle of a paragraph too.

This example may help you think of main ideas:

$$8 \quad + \quad 9 \quad + \quad 7 \quad = \quad 24$$

detail + detail + detail = main idea

The 8, 9, and 7 are like details. They are smaller than their sum, 24. The 24, like the main idea, is bigger. It is made up of several smaller parts.

Try It!

Read the following story. Then underline the main idea sentence.

Ostriches will eat anything. These birds eat grass, but they also eat wood, stones, bones, and gold. In South Africa, ostriches are hunted for the diamonds that they may swallow. Ostriches in zoos have been known to eat wallets, watches, keys, and coins.

The main idea sentence is the first sentence about ostriches. The other sentences are details. They give examples of what the main idea sentence states.

The main idea could come at the end of the paragraph:

Ostriches eat grass, but they also eat wood, stones, bones, and gold. In South Africa, ostriches are hunted for the diamonds they may swallow. Ostriches in zoos have been known to eat wallets, watches, keys, and coins. Ostriches will eat anything.

Practice Finding the Main Idea

This unit asks you to find the main ideas of paragraphs. For example, read the paragraph and answer the question below.

The people of ancient Egypt created an advanced civilization. More than 6,000 years ago, they developed a calendar with 360 days divided into 12 months. The people made paper and learned to write. They built huge monuments with machines they invented.

_B_ 1. The story mainly tells
    A. how people made paper
    B. about the creation of Egyptian civilization
    C. where an ancient calendar was invented
    D. how the people built monuments

The correct answer is B. The first sentence says, "The people of ancient Egypt created an advanced civilization." This is the main idea sentence. It tells what the people did. The other sentences are details. They tell how the Egyptians were an advanced society.

Sometimes a story does not have a main idea sentence. It is made up only of details. You put all the details together to find the main idea. Read the story below and answer the question. Write the letter of your answer on the blank line.

Microchips provide the power for wristwatches. They are also the brains in our computers, and they control robots. These chips are used in video games and space shuttles. They make our cameras, radios, and televisions small and light.

_____ 2. The story mainly tells
    A. how computers work
    B. why televisions are small
    C. how microchips are used
    D. how cameras are made

Read each passage. After each passage you will answer a question about the main idea of the passage. Remember, the main idea is the main point in a story.

1. Imagine testing glass by throwing chickens at it! Sometimes fast-moving airplanes fly through flocks of birds. If the birds hit the windshield of a plane, the glass could shatter and cause a crash. Airplane manufacturers have made a chicken cannon that fires rubber chickens at glass windshields. If the windshield doesn't break when the rubber chicken hits it, the designers know that the glass can withstand the force of a real crash.

_____ 1. The story mainly tells
  A. why birds can be dangerous to airplanes
  B. how a chicken cannon tests glass
  C. how big a bird has to be to damage an airplane
  D. how the chicken cannon works

2. The harmless hognose snake is a champion bluffer. When this snake is threatened, it hisses and acts as if it will bite. If you don't run away, the hognose snake "plays dead." It rolls over on its back, wiggling around as if it's in distress. Then it "dies" with its mouth open and tongue hanging out. If you turn it on its stomach, the snake will roll over on its back again.

_____ 2. The story mainly tells
  A. where the hognose snake is found
  B. what things frighten the hognose snake
  C. how dangerous the hognose snake is
  D. how the hognose snake bluffs

3. Doctors think that wearing red-tinted glasses can relieve sadness. Some people get very moody and sad in the winter. They may be affected by the brief days. Bright lights help some people but not everyone. The reddish light coming through rose-colored glasses seems to make people feel happy.

_____ **3.** The story mainly tells
    A. why happy people wear rose-colored glasses
    B. when some people get sad
    C. how short the daylight is in winter
    D. how colored glasses may help people feel better

---

4. The Marines had a problem in World War II. Orders were sent in code, but the enemy kept learning the code. Nothing could be kept secret. Then someone thought that Navajo soldiers could help the Marines. Since very few other people could speak Navajo, this language was used as a code. No one on the enemy side knew Navajo, so the messages stayed secret.

_____ **4.** The story mainly tells
    A. how Navajo people kept secrets
    B. when the secret code was used
    C. how the Marines used Navajo as a code
    D. why the original code had to be changed

---

5. Dogs have been called our best friends, but they are also good helpers. They can be used in many ways. Some dogs hunt while others guard animals and property. Boxers and German shepherds are trained to lead people who are blind. A dog named Laika was the first animal in space.

_____ **5.** The story mainly tells
    A. how many types of dogs there are
    B. what the name of the space dog was
    C. what kind of dogs can lead people who are blind
    D. how dogs are useful

1. Tap dancing started in America. It began as folk dancing that had much kicking and stamping. Over time two kinds of dancing developed. In one kind the dancers wore hard shoes and danced very fast. In the other they wore soft shoes and danced slowly and easily. There wasn't really any *tap* in tap dancing until 1925. That's when someone put metal pieces on the toes and heels of tap shoes.

_____ **1.** The story mainly tells
    A. how there are two kinds of tap dancing
    B. how tap shoes are made
    C. where some folk dances came from
    D. how tap dancing developed

2. Trousers are a recent style in the history of fashion. Men wore tights under short, loose pants until the early 1800s when the first real pants for men appeared. Until the 1940s few women wore long pants. During World War II, women factory workers started wearing long pants. The fashion caught on.

_____ **2.** The story mainly tells
    A. that long pants are a somewhat new fashion
    B. when men stopped wearing pantaloons
    C. who wore tights
    D. why women don't wear trousers

3. When you take a multiple-choice test, do you ever change your answers? Some scientists think that it is a smart thing to do. They found out that most students who change their answers make the right decision and make better scores on their tests.

_____ **3.** The story mainly tells
    A. how to study for tests
    B. what scientists think about answers
    C. how to score better on a multiple-choice test
    D. which answers to change on tests

4. It takes more than food to make babies grow up to be healthy and happy. If babies are not patted and hugged, they grow more slowly and are less healthy. Also they will not be as smart or as happy when they become adults. Many studies show that love is the most important thing in children's lives.

_____ **4.** The story mainly tells
  A. why good food is important to babies
  B. what makes babies grow up
  C. that children need love to grow up healthy
  D. how to have smart children

---

5. Probably the best-known rodeo cowboy in the world is Larry Mahan. Mahan was the national champion six times before he was 30. He was good at every event and was so successful that he had his own plane. When he got too old to be in the rodeo, he didn't stop doing rodeo work. He started a rodeo school.

_____ **5.** The story mainly tells
  A. where to ride bulls and rope calves
  B. about the most famous rodeo cowboy in the world
  C. how to get rich in the rodeo
  D. where to go to rodeo school

1. The lack of gravity in space makes even simple tasks a challenge. Astronauts have to wear boots that hold their feet to the floor so that they can walk around. Eating is a real chore. Dried and frozen foods are stored in plastic bags. To eat chicken soup, the astronauts cut a hole in one end of the bag and squeeze the soup into their mouths.

_____ **1.** The story mainly tells
   A. why there is little gravity in space
   B. why easy tasks are challenging in space
   C. why space food is stored in plastic bags
   D. how to eat chicken soup

2. "The War of the Worlds," a radio story, once started a panic. Because many people didn't hear that it was just a story about monsters from space, they thought the fake news bulletins were true. People were frantic. It took hours to calm them down and convince them that it was only a radio play.

_____ **2.** The story mainly tells
   A. what people thought about news stories
   B. why people were afraid of the monsters
   C. how a radio play fooled many people
   D. where the monsters in the story came from

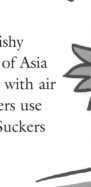
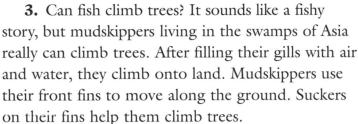

3. Can fish climb trees? It sounds like a fishy story, but mudskippers living in the swamps of Asia really can climb trees. After filling their gills with air and water, they climb onto land. Mudskippers use their front fins to move along the ground. Suckers on their fins help them climb trees.

_____ **3.** The story mainly tells
- **A.** where mudskippers live
- **B.** how they fill their gills
- **C.** how mudskippers can climb trees
- **D.** where mudskippers have suckers

4. The peanut is a humble plant with hundreds of functions. Most peanuts are roasted in their shells and lightly salted. About half the peanuts eaten in the United States are ground into a thick paste called peanut butter. The rich oil made from peanuts is good for frying foods and is used for oiling machines and making soaps and paint. Even peanut shells are used to make plastics and to fertilize soil.

_____ **4.** The story mainly tells
- **A.** why peanut oil is used for frying
- **B.** how much peanut butter is eaten in the United States
- **C.** about the many uses of the peanut
- **D.** why peanut shells make good fertilizer

5. Some college teachers in Michigan have made a small computer that looks like an orange. It will be picked and handled like real fruit. Since much fruit is damaged on its way to market, this machine will measure shaking and temperature changes. The computerized orange will help people find ways to avoid damaging fruits during shipping.

_____ **5.** The story mainly tells
- **A.** where the computerized orange was created
- **B.** how the computer company helped make the machine
- **C.** what the computerized orange looks like
- **D.** about the purpose of the computerized orange

1. There are many ways to learn about people. You can learn a lot about people by simply watching or talking to them. Looking at the floor can also give you information about people. You can tell where people walk most frequently because of the worn carpet. The next time you're riding in someone else's car, notice the music on the radio. The type of music played on the station can tell a lot about the person!

_____ **1.** The story mainly tells
    A. how to guess where people walk
    B. how to learn about people
    C. how to listen to the radio
    D. how to watch people

---

2. A scientist believes that millions of animals have died every 26 million years. He thinks that comets are responsible for those deaths. Comets would explode on impact as they slammed into Earth. Dust from the explosions blocked light and heat from the Sun. Plants and animals on Earth could not withstand such conditions, so they died.

_____ **2.** The story mainly tells
    A. how often animals died
    B. why comets may come near Earth
    C. where the dust comes from
    D. about a possible cause of animal deaths in the past

---

3. The diamond is a hard element that can cut through almost any metal. That is why it is often used for industrial purposes. Whole diamond stones are set into tools. Dust from crushed diamond stones is used for coating the edges of tools. Care must be taken when exposing diamonds to extreme heat because heat can turn them into graphite. Graphite is the soft material used in the manufacture of lead for pencils.

_____ **3.** The story mainly tells
    A. how to turn a diamond into graphite
    B. how diamonds are used in industry
    C. how diamond dust coats tool edges
    D. when diamonds are used in pencils

4. Many people in India don't eat beef, but they still find many uses for cattle. Cows provide milk for drinking and for other dairy products. Young cattle are used for plowing fields and carrying big loads.

_____ **4.** The story mainly tells
    A. how cows are used in India
    B. where some people do not eat beef
    C. which cows plow fields
    D. what milk is used for

---

5. Fabergé, a jeweler, made eggs from rare metals and jewels. A Russian emperor liked them so much that he often gave them away as gifts. The elaborate eggs are only a few inches high. Some have tiny clocks inside them. Others hold small pictures or toys. The highest price ever paid for a Fabergé egg was more than $5.5 million!

_____ **5.** The story mainly tells
    A. what Fabergé eggs are like
    B. who bought and gave the eggs as gifts
    C. what Fabergé eggs have in them
    D. how Fabergé made the eggs

1. Computers have changed quite a bit through the years. An early model could add 18 million numbers per hour. One person would have needed many years to do the same job. A modern computer can add 1 ½ trillion numbers in less than three hours.

_____ **1.** The story mainly tells
- **A.** who uses computers
- **B.** how long one person takes to do a job
- **C.** how computers have gotten faster over time
- **D.** how fast modern computers can add

2. Dolley Madison was the wife of President James Madison. She was quite a brave First Lady. When the White House burned down, Dolley rescued important government papers. She also saved the portrait of George Washington that hangs in the East Room today.

_____ **2.** The story mainly tells
- **A.** who Dolley Madison's husband was
- **B.** how the White House burned down
- **C.** about Dolley Madison's courageous acts
- **D.** where the portrait of George Washington hangs

3. Ages ago living things like bugs and leaves got trapped in soft tree resin. The resin hardened into what we know as amber. It kept the trapped bugs and leaves in perfect shape. Now scientists are learning much about the distant past from amber samples. Some scientists say they are more useful than fossils.

_____ **3.** The story mainly tells
  A. where bugs and leaves got trapped
  B. what hard resin is called
  C. why amber samples are important to scientists
  D. what scientists think of fossils

4. The beaver's front teeth have a hard, bright-orange covering. These teeth are used to cut and tear the bark off trees. The back teeth are flat and rough and are used for chewing. There are two flaps of skin between the front and back teeth. These flaps keep water and splinters from entering the beaver's mouth.

_____ **4.** The story mainly tells
  A. about the color of the front teeth
  B. how the two flaps of skin are used
  C. about the specially designed mouth of the beaver
  D. how splinters get into the beaver's mouth

5. Product codes on items consist of bars and numbers on the product label. The first numbers tell which company made the item. The last numbers identify the product and size. A laser reads the bars at the checkout. A computer finds the price for that product and prints the price on the cash-register slip. Store owners can change prices of items by changing the computer. The records in the computer help the owners learn which goods sell well.

_____ **5.** The story mainly tells
  A. how the product codes are developed
  B. how the product-code system is effective
  C. how one machine reads the numbers and bars
  D. how the numbers are assigned to companies

1. Native Americans dried strips of meat, pounded it into a paste, and then mixed it with fat. Sometimes they added berries and sugar. Then they pressed it into small cakes. They called these cakes pemmican. Pemmican didn't spoil, and it provided lots of energy for people traveling or going hunting. Today explorers still carry and eat this food.

_____ **1.** The story mainly tells
- **A.** who uses pemmican today
- **B.** what can be put into pemmican
- **C.** how pemmican was prepared by Native Americans
- **D.** why people eat pemmican today

2. Because lambs are sometimes eaten by coyotes, ranchers may hunt or trap the coyotes. However, killing coyotes may upset nature's balance. Scientists have found a way to protect sheep without killing coyotes. Coyotes are fed lamb meat treated with a drug. When they eat the meat, they get sick. Later, coyotes won't even go near lambs. They'll hunt rabbits instead.

_____ **2.** The story mainly tells
- **A.** why coyotes prefer rabbits to lambs
- **B.** why killing coyotes upsets nature's balance
- **C.** how scientists protect sheep and coyotes
- **D.** what kind of people do not like coyotes

3. The spots on a fawn's coat let it hide in shady areas without being seen. The viceroy butterfly looks like the bad-tasting monarch, so birds avoid both. The hognose snake hisses and rolls on its back when it fears another animal. When the opossum is attacked, it plays dead. Distressed turtles hide in their shells until they're sure it's safe to come out again.

_____ **3.** The story mainly tells
- **A.** how some animals protect themselves
- **B.** why some harmless animals look dangerous
- **C.** why spots or stripes make animals less visible
- **D.** why birds don't like monarch butterflies

4. For years food chemists have tasted hot peppers used for chili sauce, catsup, and pizza, but people had a hard time figuring out the spiciness of the peppers. After eating two or three, their taste buds were burning. Now a machine can test different kinds of hot peppers. It measures the chemicals that provide the spicy taste of the peppers.

_____ **4.** The story mainly tells
     A. how scientists measure chemicals
     B. how hot and spicy peppers are used
     C. why people have trouble tasting hot peppers
     D. how a machine helps the hot-pepper industry

---

5. The temperature in Antarctica once fell to 128 degrees below zero Fahrenheit. In the summertime, temperatures average well below freezing. Most of the land is covered with ice that is up to 2 miles thick. Only a few strong mosses and sturdy spiders can live on this big block of ice. Since very little snow or rain falls there, Antarctica is a desert.

_____ **5.** The story mainly tells
     A. about a desert with extremely cold temperatures
     B. which plants and insects live in Antarctica
     C. how much snow and rain fall there
     D. how low the temperature once fell

1. The rare Chinese panda lives on tender, young bamboo shoots. Most bamboo plants die right after flowering. Without the bamboo the pandas starve. Because some people fear that the rare pandas may die out, in some places food is given to the hungry animals. Some pandas are airlifted to places where bamboo is still plentiful.

_____ **1.** The story mainly tells
     A. what the Chinese pandas usually eat
     B. how the bamboo plants flower
     C. how people are keeping pandas alive
     D. why pandas sometimes starve to death

---

2. Air plants, such as mosses and lichens, grow on buildings and stones and get their food and water from the air around them. Other plants such as mistletoe get their food and water from the trees they live on. Sometimes these trees die if the plants take away too much food or water.

_____ **2.** The story mainly tells
     A. what kinds of plants grow on buildings
     B. why mistletoe sometimes kills trees
     C. how some plants don't live in soil
     D. how mosses and lichens get food and water

3. Alfred Nobel invented dynamite to help builders, but it was used for war, which made him feel very guilty about the misuse of his invention. He was a rich man, so he set up a $9 million fund. Today the fund is used to reward people who have improved human life. Nobel Prizes are awarded in six fields, including peace, medicine, and chemistry.

_____ **3.** The story mainly tells
- **A.** what the Nobel Prizes are awarded for
- **B.** why Nobel founded the Nobel Prize fund
- **C.** how much money was set aside for rewards
- **D.** what invention Alfred Nobel created

---

4. Bob Geldof talked to the top musical talents of the world and asked them to sing at a concert to raise money. The stars agreed. Geldof found a stadium, arranged for TV coverage, and set up a trust fund. He said that none of the stars would get special treatment. Everyone would work together. In 1985, the Live Aid concert raised more than $100 million for starving children.

_____ **4.** The story mainly tells
- **A.** how Geldof found a stadium
- **B.** how many musical stars agreed to sing
- **C.** why people are hungry in Africa
- **D.** how a concert benefited starving children

---

5. In real life, rattlesnakes try to avoid people and seldom attack. Most people are bitten only after they step on these snakes. A rattlesnake may not even inject its poison when it bites. In fact, more Americans die from insect stings than from snakebites!

_____ **5.** The story mainly tells
- **A.** how rattlesnakes aren't as dangerous as everyone believes
- **B.** why insects kill people
- **C.** when rattlesnakes use their poison
- **D.** how snakes bite

1. Every year hungry deer do millions of dollars' worth of damage to young pine trees. Scientists in Washington have found a way to protect the trees. They use a substance called selenium. Selenium produces a bad smell when dissolved. A bit of this element is put in the ground near trees. Rain dissolves the selenium, and the trees absorb it. The bad smell keeps the deer away until the trees are fully grown.

_____ **1.** The story mainly tells
    A. how much damage deer do to trees
    B. how trees can be protected from deer
    C. what selenium is
    D. why deer eat pine trees

---

2. Kitty O'Neil wanted to become a stunt person. She performed incredible stunts, such as 100-foot falls. O'Neil has been deaf since birth. She says she can concentrate better than most people who can hear. She is not bothered by the sounds around her.

_____ **2.** The story mainly tells
    A. when O'Neil fell 100 feet
    B. how long O'Neil has been deaf
    C. how O'Neil's disability has helped her career
    D. how to become a stunt person

---

3. Virginia Hamilton started writing at a young age. People in her family were great storytellers. She loved to listen to their tales about her African American heritage. When she grew up, Hamilton brought the tales to life in stories. Now she is a famous writer of books for children.

_____ **3.** The story mainly tells
    A. when Virginia Hamilton started writing
    B. how Hamilton's family told stories
    C. how family stories led to a writing career
    D. what kind of tales Hamilton's family told

4. Sharks have a keen sense of hearing and can smell blood from almost 2,000 yards away. Sharks also have a special system of channels in their skin that helps them feel the vibrations of a splashing swimmer. We know that in clear water, sharks can see dinner from about 50 feet away. If you ever spot a shark, always swim away smoothly!

_____ **4.** The story mainly tells
  A. how well sharks hear
  B. why sharks have poor vision
  C. how sharks sense food
  D. when to swim away smoothly

---

5. Garlic is one of the ingredients that makes pasta sauce taste so good. Now doctors think garlic has healing powers, too. Early tests show that it can kill harmful germs. Garlic also has been found to have a good effect on the blood. Doctors think it can help protect people against heart disease.

_____ **5.** The story mainly tells
  A. how garlic can help keep people healthy
  B. what goes into pasta sauce
  C. how garlic kills harmful bacteria
  D. how garlic affects the blood

Writing Roundup

Read each paragraph. Think about the main idea. Write the main idea in your own words.

1. In France, people like to eat a mushroomlike food called truffles. Truffles are not easy to find because they grow underground. Some people in France train pigs to find the right place to dig. The pigs can smell the truffles even though they are deep in the soil.

What is main idea of this paragraph?

_____

_____

2. A ballet that tells a story was not always performed the way we see such ballets now. Long ago only men were in the dance groups, and they wore masks when they danced the women's parts. The audiences were not fooled by these men playing women's parts.

What is the main idea of this paragraph?

_____

_____

_____

_____

3. Jan Matzeliger came to the United States from Africa. He worked as a shoemaker. This gave him the idea for a shoe-shaping machine. He sold the idea to others. The machine greatly increased shoe production. Matzeliger died in 1889. Sadly, few people knew that he had invented the machine until later.

What is the main idea of this paragraph?

_____

_____

Prewriting

Think of a main idea that you would like to write about, such as a great invention, a country you'd like to visit, or something you might train your pet to do. Fill in the chart below.

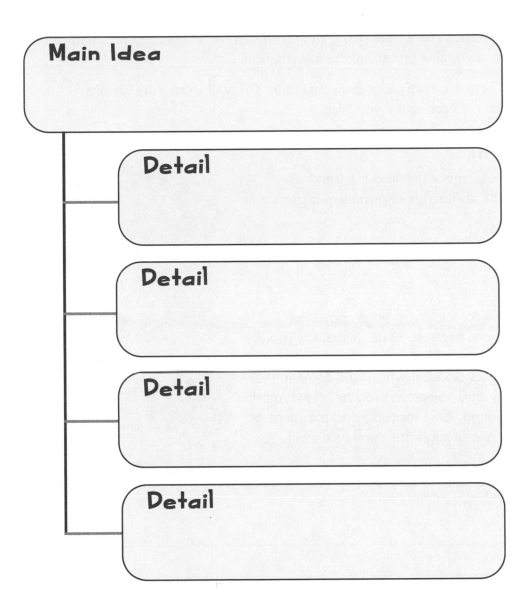

Main Idea

Detail

Detail

Detail

Detail

On Your Own

Now use another sheet of paper to write your paragraph. Underline the sentence that tells the main idea.

unit 5

What Is a Conclusion?

A conclusion is a decision you make after thinking about all the information you have. The writer may not state his or her conclusions in a story. As you read, you often have to hunt for clues. These help you understand the whole story. By putting all the clues together, you can draw a conclusion about the information.

There are many stories in this unit. You will draw conclusions based on each story you read.

Try It!

Read this story about tornadoes. Think about the information it gives you.

A tornado is a huge, powerful storm. Because of its shape, the rapidly spinning cloud is sometimes called a funnel cloud. It whirls and spins in the sky and sometimes touches down on the ground. One tornado drove a piece of straw through the trunk of a tree!

What conclusion can you draw about tornadoes? Write your conclusion on the lines below.

_____

_____

You might have written something such as, "Tornadoes can cause much destruction," or "Tornadoes can be very dangerous." You can draw these conclusions from the story. The first sentence says that a tornado is a very powerful storm. This conclusion is supported by the example in the last sentence. The third sentence tells you that these dangerous storms sometimes touch the ground. From these clues you can draw the conclusions above.

Using What You Know

Read each story on this page. Hunt for clues that will help you draw a conclusion about the location of the person telling each story.

1. I'm wearing a new suit. My hair is nicely combed. I got lost on my way here, but I drove around until I found it. I tucked a few papers into my briefcase. I took a few deep breaths, put on my best smile, and opened the office door. I really hope to get this job.

Where am I? _____

2. The first thing I do is drop some coins into a slot. Then I hold and point a hose at the car. The water comes out in a powerful spray, so I have to be careful not to put my hand in it. I can choose from cycles such as soap, rinse, and wax.

Where am I? _____

3. A few cars zoom by. Then a noisy bus passes. If only the light would hurry up and change. I must return the books before the library closes.

Where am I? _____

4. All I can hear is the wind. There isn't any traffic here. The air is very thin at this altitude. I try to take deep breaths. I think I'll have a snack before I climb any higher. I'm near the top, and I can see down into the valley, but I won't make it to the peak before lunchtime.

Where am I? _____

Read each passage. After each passage you will answer a question that will require you to draw a conclusion about the story. Remember, a conclusion is a decision you make after putting together all the clues you are given.

1. Doug Seuss trains bears to wreck cabins and chase actors in the movies. The animal trainer believes that the beasts are affectionate and smart. He romps in the creek with his 1,300-pound friend, Bart. Bart rides in the back of Doug's pickup truck to the car wash. That's where Bart takes a bath.

_____ **1.** From this story you can tell that
    A. bears don't take baths often
    B. Bart doesn't like pickups
    C. Doug is probably a good animal trainer
    D. Bart weighs less than Doug

2. The abacus is an ancient device made of beads that slide on sticks. It is widely thought that the abacus was used by storekeepers and money changers only in Asia. In fact, the abacus was also used in ancient Rome and Greece. The Russian scientists who launched the spacecraft _Sputnik_ also used an abacus to do their calculations.

_____ **2.** From the story you can tell that an abacus
    A. is used to print money
    B. is used to do math
    C. is an invention of the Greeks
    D. is no longer used today

3. In the 1800s two brothers were traveling west in a covered wagon. They grew to detest each other so much that one brother sawed the wagon in half and drove away. He left his brother stranded on the prairie with the back half of the wagon and one set of oxen.

_____ **3.** The stranded brother probably
- **A.** was angry
- **B.** bought a car
- **C.** read some books
- **D.** was sleepy

4. A gorilla named Koko learned sign language. One day Koko pulled two fingers across her cheeks to indicate whiskers. She wanted a kitten. She was given one that she named All Ball. Koko cuddled and stroked All Ball just as a mother gorilla would stroke a baby gorilla. She dressed All Ball in linen napkins and hats. Koko and All Ball also tickled each other. How did Koko feel about All Ball? "Soft, good cat cat," she said in sign language.

_____ **4.** You can tell from the story that
- **A.** kittens like to wear hats
- **B.** Koko hates to tickle animals
- **C.** gorillas can be loving and intelligent
- **D.** baby gorillas have whiskers

5. Thomas Jefferson's home, Monticello, is famous. Many people visited the president there and Jefferson could not turn guests away. He had another home near Lynchburg, Virginia. It was called Poplar Forest, and Jefferson went there when Monticello got too crowded.

_____ **5.** For Jefferson, Poplar Forest was a place
- **A.** to get away from the heat at Monticello
- **B.** where he could be a real farmer
- **C.** he liked better than Monticello
- **D.** to be alone

1. The planet Saturn is famous for the rings around it. The rings are made of tiny pieces of matter floating around the planet. The space ship *Voyager 2* has shown that gravity pulls the pieces away from the ring. They fall toward Saturn. As more pieces fall, there appears to be less of a ring.

_____ **1.** This story suggests that
    A. Saturn may not always have its rings
    B. Saturn is the only planet to have rings
    C. *Voyager 2* changed the rings of Saturn
    D. gravity keeps the rings in place

2. Weather experts can predict rain, snow, and sunshine fairly well. Now scientists can predict where lightning will strike. They can warn airplane pilots to change their routes. Also, people in charge of golf tournaments can adjust the playing schedule.

_____ **2.** From this story you can tell that
    A. experts can predict when lightning will strike
    B. airplanes aren't affected by lightning
    C. experts are usually in charge of tournaments
    D. lightning is a common danger at golf tournaments

3. The American tarantula is a large, hairy spider. It scares most people when they see it. Fortunately, the spider's bite is harmless, but it can be painful.

_____ **3.** From this story you can tell that
    A. tarantulas move fast
    B. all people are afraid of tarantulas
    C. tarantulas sting many people
    D. most people try to avoid tarantulas

4. In 1791, surgeon George Hamilton went down with a ship off the coast of Australia. Years later when divers examined the wreck, they found the doctor's silver pocket watch stopped at 12 minutes past 11. They also found a small bottle with an oily liquid in it. It contained oil of cloves used by the doctor. The liquid was still fragrant after almost 200 years in the ocean.

_____ **4.** From the story you can conclude that
    A. glass helps preserve liquids under water
    B. surgeon Hamilton had many children
    C. the divers found the wreck at 11:12 P.M.
    D. small bottles hold liquids better than big bottles

---

5. The male bowerbird of Australia courts his mate inside a colorful bower, or playhouse. First the bird builds a kind of castle made of towers, huts, and pathways. He decorates this den with butterfly wings, flowers, shells, and stones. Then he waits for the female bowerbird to admire his work.

_____ **5.** You can tell that the male bowerbird
    A. cannot fly very far
    B. builds its bower to keep out the rain and heat
    C. is a coastal bird that eats fish
    D. builds its bower to attract a mate

1. Tomatoes used to be considered poisonous, perhaps because of their bright color. In 1820, a man in Salem, New Jersey, proved that they weren't harmful. Robert Johnson ate an entire basket of tomatoes in front of the whole town. His doctor was there and was sure that Johnson would die.

_____ **1.** From this story you can tell that
  A. some brightly colored plants are poisonous
  B. tomatoes are usually dull looking
  C. Johnson was afraid he would die
  D. Johnson's doctor liked tomatoes

2. Only one president has been stopped for speeding while holding office. A police officer stopped Ulysses S. Grant when he was driving a horse and buggy too fast. This was not even Grant's first offense. He was fined $5 twice before for breaking the speed limit.

_____ **2.** From this story you can tell that
  A. Grant was stopped for speeding five times
  B. speed limits were in use before cars were invented
  C. Grant had a special reason for speeding
  D. the speed limit was 5 miles per hour then

3. There is actually a summer camp for dogs in New York. The counselors hold treasure hunts for dogs by hiding dog biscuits. The camp sends regular reports about the dogs to their owners. Each report is signed with the dog's paw print.

_____ **3.** You can conclude that the dogs probably
   A. learn weaving and crafts on rainy days
   B. get homesick often
   C. are owned by people who treat their dogs like children
   D. are taught tricks by the counselors

---

4. Mechanical clocks are about 700 years old, but daily time was measured as many as 3,000 years ago. The ancient Egyptians measured time with a shadow stick. It cast a shadow across markers as the sun moved. Another "clock" was a candle marked with numbers.

_____ **4.** You can tell from the story that
   A. you can use a shadow stick at night
   B. the Egyptians were interested in mechanical clocks
   C. measuring time has interested people for ages
   D. people have always measured time with candles

---

5. Many people believe that margarine was invented during World War II. This substitute for butter was actually made by the French in 1869. It wasn't used widely in the United States because dairy farmers were against its sale. Wisconsin had the last law against it. That law ended in 1967.

_____ **5.** You can tell from the story that
   A. dairy farmers approved of the use of margarine
   B. Wisconsin probably had many dairy farmers
   C. French dairy farmers opposed the use of margarine
   D. margarine was widely used in America before 1967

1. Most people are afraid of something. A study was conducted to determine the things that people fear most. The research found that men and women tend to have the same fears. The basic difference is the order in which they rate these fears. For example, men fear bats and speaking in public the most. Women fear fire, dead people, and rats the most.

_____ **1.** From the story you can tell that
  A. male and female fears are alike and yet different
  B. everyone likes rats
  C. women fear bats more than men do
  D. everyone is afraid of chickens

2. Sarah Winnemucca worked to protect Native American rights. Her father was a chief of the Paiute tribe in Nevada. As a child she moved to California, where she lived with a white family. She attended school and learned to speak English. As an adult she became a teacher and tried to make peace between the white settlers and her native tribe. She even met to discuss the situation with President Hayes.

_____ **2.** From the story you <u>cannot</u> tell
  A. where Winnemucca's tribe lived
  B. that Winnemucca spoke English
  C. the name of Winnemucca's father
  D. what Winnemucca did as an adult

3. Man o' War was a wonderful racehorse. He won 20 of 21 races and set five world records. When Man o' War died in 1947, his owner Samuel Riddle had him buried. Riddle, who died in 1963, remembered the horse in his last will and testament. He left $4,000,000 to maintain Man o' War's grave.

_____ **3.** From the story you <u>cannot</u> tell
  A. when Man o' War died
  B. how many races Man o' War won
  C. when Samuel Riddle died
  D. where Man o' War is buried

4. William Pace was a pig farmer in Mississippi. He didn't raise his pigs in the ordinary way. Instead of letting the pigs wallow in the mud and heat, he fattened the creatures in the barn by using a giant fan and a TV set. Pace believed that the pigs were happier if they could watch television. The pigs' favorite show seemed to be wrestling!

_____ **4.** You can conclude that William Pace
- **A.** thought happy pigs grew fatter
- **B.** used regular ways to raise pigs
- **C.** lived in Missouri
- **D.** trained his pigs to wrestle

---

5. In the 1800s miners carried canaries into the mines with them. The canaries not only provided music but also served an important purpose. If the birds stopped singing, it was a signal to the miners that there was little oxygen left in the mine.

_____ **5.** The story suggests that canaries
- **A.** were good miners
- **B.** needed enough air to sing
- **C.** were useless to the miners
- **D.** needed darkness to sing

1. Restaurants come in many shapes in Los Angeles, California. One building looks like a large chili bowl. Another one is shaped like a hot dog. For a fast snack, you can drive through a building that looks like two doughnuts.

_____ **1.** You can conclude that

    A. these restaurants serve the best food

    B. all the restaurants serve doughnuts

    C. these buildings were designed by cooks

    D. the shapes tell about the main food served

2. Travelers often stop to wonder at unusual buildings. There's a house made of salt in Grand Saline, Texas. Both Kentucky and Tennessee have houses built from coal. In a town in Maine, visitors gape at a building made from paper. A tour of a house in Florida tells how this house was carved from coral.

_____ **2.** You can tell that unusual houses are

    A. tourist attractions

    B. pleasant to live in

    C. not very popular

    D. usually built of wood

3. One of the deadliest fish in the world is the puffer. In Japan this fish is called fugu. Some people in Japan like to eat fugu. Cooks have been trained to remove the poisonous parts from the fish. Then they arrange the raw fish into beautiful designs and serve it. Even so, as many as 50 Japanese die from fugu poison each year.

_____ **3.** From this story you can tell that
- **A.** eating fugu is safe
- **B.** most Japanese eat fugu
- **C.** eating fugu is a daring deed
- **D.** puffers are found only in Japan

4. Scientists are working to make computers think more like people. People say things such as "add a little more." Today's computers cannot understand "little." *Little* is not a real amount. They can only understand terms such as *5 ounces.*

_____ **4.** From this story you can tell that
- **A.** computers will think like people in 20 years
- **B.** computers would not understand *a bunch*
- **C.** people think like machines
- **D.** computers give the wrong information

5. Alice Childress wrote *A Hero Ain't Nothin' but a Sandwich.* The novel tells the story of Benjie Johnson. Benjie is a 13-year-old boy. His life becomes difficult when he gets involved with the wrong people.

_____ **5.** This story does <u>not</u> tell
- **A.** who the author of the book is
- **B.** what the title of the book is
- **C.** how old Benjie is
- **D.** how Benjie solves his problems

1. Longfellow wrote a poem that made Paul Revere famous for his ride to Concord to warn that the British were coming. Actually, Revere never made it to Concord, and he did not ride alone. Two other riders, William Dawes and Dr. Samuel Prescott, went with him. It was Dr. Prescott who warned Concord about the British.

_____ **1.** From this story you <u>cannot</u> tell
  A. whether the people of Concord were warned
  B. how the people of Concord got the warning
  C. that Revere never made it to Concord
  D. whether or not Longfellow wrote a good poem

2. The United States is full of small, special museums. There is a Sport Fishing Museum in New York, a museum of locks in Connecticut, and the Maple Museum in Vermont. The Lumberman's Museum is located in Maine, and the Petrified Creatures Museum is found in New York.

_____ **2.** In the Vermont museum, you could probably find
  A. a sport fish caught by a lumberman
  B. a petrified fish
  C. maple syrup buckets
  D. a petrified lumberman

3. The parasol ant of South America gets its name from the way it carries a bit of leaf over its head. Native Brazilians call them doctor ants. They use the ants' strong jaws to clamp down on deep cuts and keep them closed. Once the jaws clamp, the Brazilians pinch off the ants' bodies to keep the wound sealed.

_____ **3.** From the story you can tell that
  A. parasol ants haven't been named correctly
  B. the ants' jaws stay closed after the ants die
  C. native Brazilians named the ants "parasol ants"
  D. the ants like sunshine

4. In 1883, a California postal carrier named Jim Stacy found a stray dog, whom he called Dorsey. Dorsey accompanied Stacy on his mail route. Stacy got sick shortly after finding Dorsey, so he tied the mail along with a note to the dog's back and sent him out alone. Dorsey delivered the mail in this fashion until 1886.

_____ **4.** From this story you can conclude that
    A. Stacy was sick for a long time
    B. Dorsey would never leave Stacy's side
    C. the note told people what to feed Dorsey
    D. Dorsey received a medal from the post office

5. The odd-looking dodo bird became extinct shortly after it was discovered. In 1598, it was found on an island by a Dutch admiral. The admiral took some birds back with him to Europe. Pictures of the dodo were painted and appeared everywhere. But by 1681, every dodo in the world had died.

_____ **5.** The story suggests that
    A. the discovery of the dodo led to its disappearance
    B. the birds were painted for their great beauty
    C. the Dutch were good painters
    D. the dodo came from Europe originally

1. Working at home sounds like fun. You can work in your pajamas, or you can play the radio as loud as you want. You can even sleep an extra hour in the morning. However, making money at home takes drive and dedication. To be successful you must use basic business practices. You must make yourself work rather than play.

_____ **1.** To be successful you would probably need to
   A. stock the refrigerator with plenty of food
   B. make a schedule and stick to it
   C. plan when to take naps
   D. work as little as possible

2. In the seventeenth century, the Incan people of South America had an empire that stretched more than 2,500 miles. They built highways throughout their empire. One of their tunnels extended 750 feet through a mountain cliff. One of their rope suspension bridges is still used today.

_____ **2.** From this story you <u>cannot</u> tell
   A. the size of the Inca Empire
   B. in what period the Inca lived
   C. if the Inca were skilled in engineering
   D. why the roads were important to the Inca

3. When the Tacoma Narrows Bridge was built in 1940, it was the world's third-largest suspension bridge. Large suspension bridges had been built before, but the builders didn't count on the winds near Tacoma, Washington. Four months after its opening, the bridge was blown down.

_____ **3.** From this story you can conclude that
    A. earlier bridges weren't in high-wind areas
    B. the Tacoma Narrows Bridge was too large
    C. high winds have little effect on suspension bridges
    D. the two larger bridges had similar problems

---

4. From news reports about Russia, you may think that the Kremlin is a large building in Moscow. Actually, there are many kremlins in Russia. *Kremlin* means "fortress" in Russian. In Moscow the Kremlin is not one building but many buildings inside a walled yard.

_____ **4.** You can tell that Moscow's Kremlin probably
    A. is the only one in Russia
    B. is a large building in Russia
    C. was originally a fortress
    D. is never visited by news reporters

---

5. The Egyptian pyramids were built from stones weighing about 2 $\frac{1}{2}$ tons each. The structures are 40 stories high. The number of stones used in each pyramid could build a wall around France. Yet the Egyptians used no animals. They had no cranes at that time. The wheel wasn't even in use.

_____ **5.** You can tell from this story that
    A. the Egyptians built a wall around France
    B. the work must have been done by many people
    C. the pyramids were 2 $\frac{1}{2}$ stories high
    D. each pyramid weighed about 2 $\frac{1}{2}$ tons

1. Ana carefully filled the bird feeders in her backyard. The many trees that grew on her property were home to various kinds of birds. Ana enjoyed watching the birds and listening to them as they came to eat the seeds she provided for them.

_____ **1.** This story does <u>not</u> tell
   A. what kind of food Ana gives the birds
   B. what kinds of birds come to the bird feeders
   C. where the bird feeders are located
   D. where the birds lived

2. The special material in our body that makes us who we are is called DNA. Except for identical twins, everybody has different DNA. Since DNA is everywhere in the body, DNA patterns are generally better than fingerprints for identifying people. Police sometimes use DNA patterns to identify suspects.

_____ **2.** From this story you can tell that
   A. some people have no DNA
   B. DNA is not found in hair
   C. fingerprints are the only way to identify people
   D. DNA patterns can help solve crimes

3. Wind does not push sailboats forward. Instead, the sailboats _fall_. The sails on the boat form a curve when the wind passes across them. The curve creates an empty space behind the sail. The boat goes forward by falling into the empty space.

_____ **3.** From this story you <u>cannot</u> tell
   A. why the sails on a sailboat form a curve
   B. how the sailboat moves forward
   C. how an empty space is created
   D. how the sails are attached to the boat

4. In a radio interview, Albert Einstein was once asked whether he got his great thoughts while relaxing in the bathtub, walking, or sitting in his office. Einstein replied, "I don't really know. I've only had one or maybe two."

_____ **4.** From this story you can tell that Einstein
- **A.** thought much like the interviewer
- **B.** enjoyed radio interviews
- **C.** thought too much value was placed on his ideas
- **D.** thought best while walking

5. A comet is like a dirty ball of snow. It is made of frozen gases, frozen water, and dust. As a comet approaches the sun, the icy center gets hot and evaporates. The gases made by the evaporation form the tail of the comet. The dust left behind in the process forms meteor showers.

_____ **5.** You can conclude from the story that
- **A.** comets are made of snow
- **B.** throwing a ball of snow can turn it into a comet
- **C.** the sun helps create the tail of the comet
- **D.** meteor showers are visible with a telescope

Writing Roundup

Read each paragraph. Think about a conclusion you can draw.
Write your conclusion in a complete sentence.

1. Polo is a game played on horseback. Each team has four players who attempt to hit a ball with their sticks. Each player has to handle the stick with his or her right hand and control the horse with the left hand. The team that scores more goals wins. Goals are scored by hitting the ball inside the other team's goalposts.

What conclusion can you draw from this paragraph?

_____

_____

2. Phillis Wheatley was born in Africa. At the age of eight, she was brought to America as a slave. There she learned English and Latin, and she managed to gain her freedom. In 1770, she published her first poem. After that she gained fame as a poet. She even shared her poetry with others when she made a trip to England in 1773.

What conclusion can you draw from this paragraph?

_____

_____

3. Alonso is building a weather station. He wants to record details about the weather in his town. So far he has a thermometer to measure air temperature, a gauge to measure rainfall, and a windsock to check wind direction. He still needs something to measure snowfall.

What conclusion can you draw from this paragraph?

_____

_____

Read the paragraph below. What conclusions can you draw? Use the clues in the paragraph to answer the questions in complete sentences.

Juneteenth is a holiday in Texas. It's also celebrated by some people in California and other western states. It can be traced back to the time Union troops arrived in Texas on June 19, 1865. They brought news that the Civil War had ended and that all the slaves were free. This put an end to slavery in Texas. Juneteenth got its name from some people in Texas who had their own way to say "June 19th." Their way stuck!

1. Is Juneteenth a holiday in all states? How do you know?

_____

_____

2. Was there slavery in Texas? How do you know?

_____

_____

3. Before the Union troops arrived, did Texans know the Civil War was over? How do you know?

_____

_____

4. Did Californians coin the word *Juneteenth*? How do you know?

_____

_____

6

What Is an Inference?

An inference is a guess you make after thinking about what you already know. For example, suppose you plan to go to the beach. From what you know about beaches, you might infer that the beach is covered with sand and the sun is shining.

An author does not write every detail in a story. If every detail were included, stories would be long and boring, and the main point would be lost. As you read, the writer expects you to fill in missing details from your own experiences. Suppose you read, "Sabrina went to the library." The writer does not have to tell you the specifics about what a library is. You already know it is a place where people go when they want to borrow books. You might infer that there are tables and chairs where people can sit and read books and magazines. People who have library cards may check out books and other materials and take them home. By filling in these missing details, you can infer that Sabrina went to the library to check out books. You can make this inference based on what you know.

Try It!

Read this story about blacksmiths, and then think about the facts.

There were many blacksmiths in colonial America. Blacksmiths spent long hours hammering the hot iron used to make tools. They made horseshoes, axes, hoes, plow blades, kettles, and pots for the townspeople. Blacksmiths who lived near shipyards made anchors, rudder irons, and tools for ships.

What inference can you make about blacksmiths? Write an inference on the line below.

_____

You might have written something such as, "Blacksmiths made most of the important tools in colonial America." You can make these inferences by putting together the facts in the story and what you already know.

Practice Making Inferences

Read each story, and then read the statements that follow. Some of the statements are facts. They can be found in the story. Other statements are inferences. Decide whether each statement is a fact or an inference. The first one has been done for you.

Rebecca's mother woke her up at 6:30. "I have to leave early for work this morning," she said. "Please get up and start dressing so you'll be ready when the bus comes." Rebecca turned over and pulled the pillow over her head.

Fact	Inference		
○	●	**1.** **A.**	Rebecca went back to sleep.
●	○	**B.**	Rebecca's mother woke her up.
○	●	**C.**	Rebecca missed the bus.
○	●	**D.**	Rebecca wasn't ready to get up.

The first sentence of the story says that Rebecca's mother woke her, so we know that **B** is a fact. You can guess that Rebecca went back to sleep, but it isn't stated in the story, so **A** is an inference. You can also guess that Rebecca missed the bus and that she wasn't ready to get up, but neither of these is stated in the story. Therefore, **C** and **D** are also inferences.

Every summer sea turtles come to the remote beaches near Boca Raton, Florida. With their large front flippers, the female turtles dig large pits in the sand and then deposit perfectly round, white eggs. The eggs have leathery shells. The female turtle pushes sand over the eggs, and then she crawls back into the ocean. Scientists take many groups of people to see the sea turtles laying their eggs.

Fact	Inference		
○	○	**2.** **A.**	Sea turtles dig large pits in the sand.
○	○	**B.**	Many people are interested in the sea turtles.
○	○	**C.**	The mother turtle does not stay with the eggs.
○	○	**D.**	The eggs have leathery shells.

Read the passages. Use what you know about inference to answer the questions. Remember, an inference is a guess you make by putting together what you know and what you read or see in the stories.

1. The construction of the Tower of Pisa began in 1174. The builders made a big mistake. They built the foundation in sand, and sand shifts frequently. Over the years the tower started to lean. It now is more than 16 feet out of line.

Fact	Inference		
○	○	**1. A.**	Modern builders don't build on sand.
○	○	**B.**	The shifting sand caused the tower to lean.
○	○	**C.**	Construction of the tower began in 1174.
○	○	**D.**	The tower now leans more than 16 feet.

2. Men and women button their clothes differently. There is a good reason for this difference. Buttons were first used to fasten clothes more than 700 years ago. Buttons were expensive then, and only rich people could buy them. Most men are right-handed, so men's clothes were made to be buttoned easily by right-handed men. In those days most rich women were dressed by their right-handed servants. The servants faced the women to button their clothes. Women's clothes had buttons on the left so they could be buttoned easily by the servants.

Fact	Inference		
○	○	**2. A.**	Buttons were first used more than 700 years ago.
○	○	**B.**	At first buttons were expensive.
○	○	**C.**	Rich men dressed themselves.
○	○	**D.**	Most rich women were dressed by servants.

3. Scientists measure the distances in space in light-years. A light-year is the distance that light travels in 365 days. A light-year is about 5,880 billion miles. The closest star to Earth is about 4.3 light-years away. That means that the light from the star took 4.3 years to reach Earth.

Fact	Inference		
○	○	**3.** **A.**	Distance in space is measured in light-years.
○	○	**B.**	The light we see from stars has traveled through space for many years.
○	○	**C.**	Light from different stars travels through space at the same speed.
○	○	**D.**	The farther away a star is, the longer it takes the light to reach Earth.

4. Rodney bragged to his friends that he could find his way around anywhere. One day, though, Rodney was delivering pizza in a strange part of town. Though he searched for half an hour, he could not locate the address. Finally he had to stop to ask for directions. His face turned red, and he stuttered as he asked how to find the place.

Fact	Inference		
○	○	**4.** **A.**	Rodney didn't have a city map.
○	○	**B.**	Asking for directions embarrassed Rodney.
○	○	**C.**	Rodney delivered pizzas.
○	○	**D.**	Rodney searched for half an hour.

5. The Civil War ended in 1865. The two opposing generals, Ulysses S. Grant and Robert E. Lee, met to discuss the terms of surrender. The site was a small town in Virginia called Appomattox Courthouse. The meeting was quiet and short, and they soon agreed to the terms. Afterward Grant said he was not overjoyed by the end of the war. Instead Grant felt sad Lee had lost. Grant respected Lee as a man who fought bravely for a cause he believed in.

Fact	Inference		
○	○	**5.** **A.**	The Civil War ended in 1865.
○	○	**B.**	Lee felt the terms were fair.
○	○	**C.**	Lee and Grant met in Virginia.
○	○	**D.**	Grant felt sad that Lee had lost.

1. John Milton was one of England's greatest poets, but at the age of 44 he went blind. Since Milton could no longer write, he had to tell his poems to his daughter, who wrote them down. This method was slow and tiring. Milton's greatest poem, *Paradise Lost*, was long and took many months to complete.

Fact	Inference		
○	○	**1.** **A.**	John Milton was a poet.
○	○	**B.**	Milton's daughter was very helpful.
○	○	**C.**	John Milton went blind.
○	○	**D.**	Milton's greatest poem was *Paradise Lost*.

2. Mary worked as a cook in a cafe. One day she got the great idea to cook the world's largest pancake. For days she worked to build a giant frying pan. Then she mixed pancake batter all night long. When she poured the batter in the pan and heard the familiar sizzle, she knew her idea had worked.

Fact	Inference		
○	○	**2.** **A.**	Mary worked in a cafe.
○	○	**B.**	Mary wanted to do something unusual.
○	○	**C.**	She cooked the world's largest pancake.
○	○	**D.**	The large pancake made Mary famous.

3. Roy Campanella was a baseball catcher for the Brooklyn Dodgers. He was named the best player in the National League three times. His career came to a halt suddenly in 1958 when he was paralyzed in a car wreck.

Fact	Inference		
○	○	**3.** **A.**	Roy Campanella was a catcher.
○	○	**B.**	The Dodgers played in Brooklyn.
○	○	**C.**	Campanella was in a car wreck in 1958.
○	○	**D.**	His injuries were very serious.

4. The hare thought he was a pretty fast fellow. One day he thought he would have some fun, so he challenged the tortoise to a race. Much to the hare's delight, the tortoise accepted the challenge. When the day of the race arrived, the hare quickly got ahead and decided to take a nap. The tortoise kept up a slow, steady pace and soon passed the sleeping hare. By the time the hare woke up, it was too late, for the steady tortoise had won the race.

Fact	Inference		
○	○	**4. A.**	The hare thought he could beat the tortoise.
○	○	**B.**	The race was between the hare and tortoise.
○	○	**C.**	The hare underestimated the tortoise.
○	○	**D.**	The tortoise won the race.

---

5. John Wesley Powell loved the American West. He liked to study its different rocks and their forms. In 1871, when he was exploring the Colorado River, he found an enormous canyon. It was later named the Grand Canyon. Powell and his group then followed the river through the canyon. Theirs was the first recorded boat trip through the Grand Canyon.

Fact	Inference		
○	○	**5. A.**	Powell explored the Colorado River.
○	○	**B.**	Powell found the Grand Canyon.
○	○	**C.**	The boat ride in the canyon was exciting.
○	○	**D.**	Powell studied rocks and their forms.

1. Janna liked to jog every day. One day as she was jogging, she spotted something in the grass, so she decided to investigate. It was a wallet full of money. Janna knew she could just keep the money and no one would ever find out about it. Janna also knew that the person who lost the wallet probably needed the money. Janna took the wallet to the police station.

Fact	Inference	
○	○	**1.** **A.** Janna was an honest person.
○	○	**B.** A wallet was lying in the grass.
○	○	**C.** The police looked for the owner of the wallet.
○	○	**D.** Jogging was one of Janna's favorite activities.

2. In Greek legends King Midas loved gold and wealth. For an act of friendship, Midas received a wish. Midas wished that everything he touched would turn to gold. The king was granted his wish, but he soon realized he had made a serious mistake when even his food and drink turned to gold.

Fact	Inference	
○	○	**2.** **A.** King Midas loved gold.
○	○	**B.** Everything Midas touched turned to gold.
○	○	**C.** King Midas was greedy.
○	○	**D.** The king didn't like his golden touch.

3. When Jim Abbott was born, part of his arm had not formed completely. He had only one working hand, but Jim made the most of his situation. In college Jim became the star pitcher of the baseball team. He played so well that he was later signed by a professional team. Jim Abbott became a major-league pitcher.

Fact	Inference	
○	○	**3. A.** Abbott overcame his disability.
○	○	**B.** People were impressed by Abbott's skill.
○	○	**C.** In college Abbott was a pitcher.
○	○	**D.** Abbott was signed by a professional team.

4. Mosquitoes are a tremendous problem in the summer. Mosquitoes love the hot weather. Then they can fly around and bite as many people as they want. Mosquitoes can't beat their wings in cool weather. The temperature must be more than 60 degrees for mosquitoes to fly.

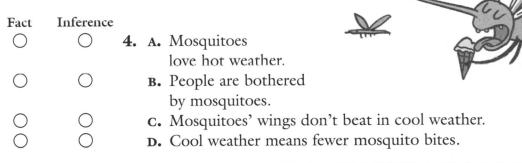

Fact	Inference	
○	○	**4. A.** Mosquitoes love hot weather.
○	○	**B.** People are bothered by mosquitoes.
○	○	**C.** Mosquitoes' wings don't beat in cool weather.
○	○	**D.** Cool weather means fewer mosquito bites.

5. Janet was waiting in line at the supermarket. The line at the checkout counter was long, and some of the customers were getting angry. The clerk was having trouble with the cash register. Janet could see that the clerk was about to cry. Finally Janet's turn came to check out. Janet paid for her purchase and smiled as the clerk returned her change. After counting the change, Janet realized the clerk had given her too much money. Janet informed the clerk, and the clerk smiled in appreciation.

Fact	Inference	
○	○	**5. A.** The customers didn't like waiting in line.
○	○	**B.** Janet was a good person.
○	○	**C.** The clerk was having a bad day.
○	○	**D.** Janet received too much change.

1. The Pig War took place in the 1880s between Great Britain and the United States. It was not really a war, just a big argument. The dispute happened on an island off the state of Washington. An American man shot a pig owned by a British man. Because of this event, the two nations were willing to go to war. In the end, the problem was solved without fighting.

Fact	Inference	
○	○	**1. A.** The Pig War took place on an island.
○	○	**B.** The man was upset that his pig was shot.
○	○	**C.** An American man shot the pig.
○	○	**D.** The two governments met to discuss the problem.

2. As the ants worked to gather food for the winter, the grasshopper enjoyed himself. He played the fiddle and took long naps. The ants warned him that he should get busy, but he ignored them. Soon winter arrived, and the grasshopper found himself hungry and miserable out in the cold.

Fact	Inference	
○	○	**2. A.** The grasshopper would rather play than work.
○	○	**B.** The ants were hard workers.
○	○	**C.** The grasshopper played the fiddle.
○	○	**D.** The ants knew food was scarce in the winter.

3. Richard Byrd was a famous American explorer. In 1930, he was in Antarctica. His party had to leave suddenly because of illness. Byrd returned to his base there three years later. Though the buildings they had used earlier were covered with ice, things inside were exactly as they had left them. A mess on a dining table remained. Food they had left was still good. Even the lights sprang to life after being off for so long.

Fact	Inference	
○	○	**3. A.** Antarctica is cold and icy.
○	○	**B.** Richard Byrd was an American explorer.
○	○	**C.** Richard Byrd was in Antarctica in 1930.
○	○	**D.** The explorers were in a hurry when they left.

4. Thaddeus Cahill knew from an early age that he wanted to invent things. He loved studying the way musical sounds are made. In 1906, he created the largest and most expensive musical instrument ever made. He gave it a long name—the Telharmonium. It was 60 feet long and weighed 200 tons. This instrument could generate many sounds that no one had ever heard before.

Fact	Inference		
○	○	**4. A.**	The instrument was the largest ever made.
○	○	**B.**	Cahill wanted to invent things.
○	○	**C.**	The instrument weighed 200 tons.
○	○	**D.**	Cahill knew a lot about instrument sounds.

---

5. As a child Jane Goodall loved to study animals and insects. She took notes on birds and bugs. She even opened a small museum for her friends. She hoped to travel to Africa when she grew up. At age 26 she got her wish and went to Kenya. She stayed in Africa and has become a famous scientist. Her field of study is the behavior of chimpanzees. Goodall has claimed her success is due to patience, courage, observation, and will power.

Fact	Inference		
○	○	**5. A.**	Jane Goodall studies chimpanzees.
○	○	**B.**	Her friends liked Goodall's museum.
○	○	**C.**	Jane Goodall enjoys her work.
○	○	**D.**	Goodall went to Kenya at age 26.

1. Tulips were first grown in Turkey. The word *tulip* comes from a Turkish word meaning *turban*. A turban is a type of scarf worn wrapped around the head. In the 1600s tulips became very popular in Holland. Single tulip bulbs were bought and sold for incredibly high prices.

Fact	Inference		
○	○	**1.** **A.**	Tulips were popular in Holland.
○	○	**B.**	Only wealthy people could buy tulips.
○	○	**C.**	The word *tulip* comes from a Turkish word.
○	○	**D.**	Tulips look similar to turbans.

2. Kristin and her younger brother Andrew were planning to surprise their parents for their anniversary. They wanted to take them out to a nice French restaurant. After considering several ways to earn money, Kristin had an idea. The next Saturday Kristin and Andrew set up a soft-pretzel and lemonade stand in the park. They sold 57 soft pretzels and 83 cups of lemonade. The money they made was more than enough for their parents' anniversary surprise.

Fact	Inference		
○	○	**2.** **A.**	Andrew is younger than Kristin.
○	○	**B.**	Kristin and Andrew like French food.
○	○	**C.**	The people at the park were thirsty.
○	○	**D.**	Kristin and Andrew sold pretzels.

3. Have you ever wondered how a remote control unit can communicate with your TV set? It looks like magic, but it can be easily explained. The remote control unit sends a signal to the television as an invisible light. Humans cannot see it, but the television can. When the television senses the light, it responds by changing the channel or adjusting the volume.

Fact   Inference

○   ○   **3. A.** Remote controls make changing channels easy.
○   ○   **B.** Remote controls send an invisible light.
○   ○   **C.** Remote controls send different signals for different channels.
○   ○   **D.** Televisions can see the invisible light.

4. In 1826, a French inventor named Joseph Niepce made the first photograph. He coated a metal plate with a special chemical. Then he exposed the plate to light for about eight hours. British inventor William Fox Talbot introduced the use of negatives 13 years later. This process allowed many photos to be made from one negative.

Fact   Inference

○   ○   **4. A.** Niepce made the first photograph.
○   ○   **B.** It was easier to make photos from negatives.
○   ○   **C.** Niepce did not use negatives.
○   ○   **D.** The metal plate was exposed for eight hours.

5. Many breeds of dogs are used for work. In some cultures dogs are used to herd sheep. The dogs keep the flock from being attacked by animals such as wolves. They also keep sheep from wandering off. Sheepdogs are known for their loyalty and gentleness.

Fact   Inference

○   ○   **5. A.** Wolves are afraid of sheepdogs.
○   ○   **B.** Sheepdogs are gentle and loyal.
○   ○   **C.** There are many breeds of dogs.
○   ○   **D.** Sheepdogs are intelligent.

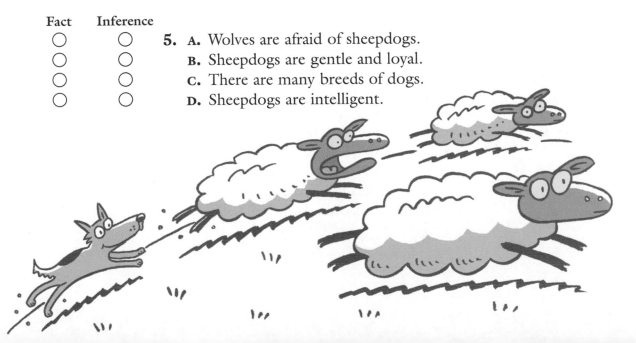

1. Sundials are an ancient way of measuring time. Experts believe they were used by the Babylonians in 2000 B.C. A sundial measures the angle of a shadow cast by the Sun. As the Sun moves from east to west during the day, so does the shadow. The shadow is cast by a flat piece of metal in the center of the dial. In the Northern Hemisphere, the metal piece must point toward the North Pole.

Fact   Inference

○   ○   **1.** **A.** Sundials measure time.
○   ○   **B.** The Sun moves from east to west.
○   ○   **C.** Sundials are useless at night.
○   ○   **D.** Time was important to the Babylonians.

---

2. Allison was upset over a difficult homework problem. She had been working on it for a while, but she still couldn't get the answer. "Why don't we go outside for a walk?" her dad suggested. Allison looked up at the stars as they walked. Her dad pointed out the planet Venus. When they returned home, Allison felt ready to tackle the homework problem. "Thanks for the walk, Dad," she said.

Fact   Inference

○   ○   **2.** **A.** The walk helped Allison calm down.
○   ○   **B.** Allison's father wanted to help her.
○   ○   **C.** Allison was doing her homework at night.
○   ○   **D.** Allison was upset over her homework.

---

3. Scott was tired from jogging, so he sat down on a park bench. He noticed a pair of glasses on the bench. When he asked several people sitting nearby whether the glasses belonged to them, they all said no. Since he couldn't find the owner, Scott decided he would take the glasses home. He put an ad in the lost and found section of the local newspaper.

Fact   Inference

○   ○   **3.** **A.** Scott was tired from jogging.
○   ○   **B.** Scott is a responsible person.
○   ○   **C.** The glasses were on the bench.
○   ○   **D.** Scott placed an ad in the paper.

4. The first band-aid was created in 1921 by Earle Dickson. He was a cotton buyer for a drug company. The bandage was designed for Dickson's wife, who frequently cut herself while cooking.

Fact	Inference		
○	○	**4. A.**	Dickson's wife frequently cut herself.
○	○	**B.**	Band-aids were created in 1921.
○	○	**C.**	Dickson worked for a drug company.
○	○	**D.**	Dickson was concerned about his wife.

5. The average weight for male cats is 8.6 pounds. The average for females is 7.2 pounds. The heaviest recorded weight for a cat is nearly 47 pounds. This cat lived in Cairns, Australia, and was named Himmy. Himmy lived to be 10 years old. The average male cat that is well fed and receives good medical care lives about 15 years.

Fact	Inference		
○	○	**5. A.**	Male cats are usually bigger than females.
○	○	**B.**	Himmy weighed nearly 47 pounds.
○	○	**C.**	An average male cat weighs 8.6 pounds.
○	○	**D.**	Himmy lived to be 10 years old.

1. The sun was just beginning to peek through the pine trees when Marisa opened her eyes. She had slept soundly in her sleeping bag all through the night. The birds sang as she got up, packed her heavy backpack, and continued the hike with the rest of her family. After two hours of steep, uphill hiking, they reached the top of the mountain. Marisa took off her backpack and sat down to smell the clean air and enjoy the view.

Fact	Inference		
○	○	**1. A.**	Marisa slept soundly.
○	○	**B.**	Marisa's family was on vacation.
○	○	**C.**	Marisa's backpack was heavy.
○	○	**D.**	Marisa enjoys hiking.

2. Stonehenge is a circle of huge stones on the Salisbury Plain in England. The average weight of each stone is 28 tons. The monument was probably built between 2800 and 2000 B.C., but no one knows who placed the stones there or what their exact purpose was. Placement of the stones made it possible to predict sunrises and sunsets, changes in the seasons, and even eclipses of the Sun and Moon.

Fact	Inference		
○	○	**2. A.**	Stonehenge is in England.
○	○	**B.**	No one is sure of Stonehenge's purpose.
○	○	**C.**	Each stone weighs about 28 tons.
○	○	**D.**	Eclipses were important to ancient people.

3. Every May across the United States, Asian Americans celebrate their cultures. May is called Asian Pacific American Heritage Month. President Bush made it official in 1990. Since then, it has grown in popularity. Today, there are parades, festivals, art shows, and workshops.

Fact	Inference		
○	○	**3. A.**	Many Americans enjoy learning about different cultures.
○	○	**B.**	The president of the United States can declare special celebrations.
○	○	**C.**	Asian Americans are proud of their heritage.
○	○	**D.**	Asian Americans celebrate in May.

4. The big homecoming dance was Friday night, and Suzanne needed a dress to wear. As she was sorting through her closet, her older sister Jean tapped her on the shoulder. She knew that Suzanne had always liked her blue dress. "How would you like to wear this?" she asked. Suzanne's eyes lit up. She hugged Jean and ran to try on the dress.

Fact	Inference		
○	○	**4. A.**	Jean was kind to her sister.
○	○	**B.**	Suzanne was excited about wearing the dress.
○	○	**C.**	The dance was Friday night.
○	○	**D.**	Jean is older than Suzanne.

5. Dragons aren't just creatures found in fairy tales. Komodo dragons are 10-foot-long lizards. They are found on the island of Komodo and other small islands in Indonesia. They have long tails and are covered with small scales. The open mouth of a Komodo dragon reveals rows of teeth that look like the edge of a saw.

Fact	Inference		
○	○	**5. A.**	Komodo dragons don't live in the United States.
○	○	**B.**	Komodo dragons have scales.
○	○	**C.**	Komodo dragons live on islands.
○	○	**D.**	Komodo dragons look very scary.

1. A limousine is a large luxury car. Most limousines are custom made. One special limousine is called "The American Dream." It is 60 feet long, has two engines, and needs two people to drive it. One person drives from the front, and the other drives from the back. The two drivers use headphones to communicate with each other.

Fact	Inference		
○	○	**1. A.**	A limousine is a car.
○	○	**B.**	"The American Dream" needs two drivers.
○	○	**C.**	It is difficult to drive "The American Dream."
○	○	**D.**	"The American Dream" has two engines.

2. Mount Vesuvius erupted in A.D. 79. The ancient city of Pompeii was buried for hundreds of years. Pompeii was a Roman port that was also an important center of business. Wealthy landowners, shopkeepers, merchants, manufacturers, and slaves lived in Pompeii. Today more than half of Pompeii has been uncovered, and visitors can get a glimpse of what life was like in the ancient Roman Empire.

Fact	Inference		
○	○	**2. A.**	Mount Vesuvius erupted in A.D. 79.
○	○	**B.**	Pompeii was buried for hundreds of years.
○	○	**C.**	Slavery was allowed in Pompeii.
○	○	**D.**	Pompeii was a large city.

3. Bill loved to explore the forest near his house. He stopped for a while to throw stones into the lake. Then he decided to hike deeper into the woods. After more than an hour of hiking, he stopped to rest. When it was time to go home, he realized he was unsure of which direction to go.

Fact	Inference		
○	○	**3. A.**	Bill is adventurous.
○	○	**B.**	The forest is near Bill's house.
○	○	**C.**	Bill threw stones into the lake.
○	○	**D.**	Bill was tired after hiking.

4. Anna had stayed up late on Thursday night to finish her model of a volcano for the science fair at school. The next morning she was late for school and did not have time to carefully pack her science project. As she started to dash across the crosswalk in front of the school, she had to stop suddenly to avoid a car she had not seen. "Oh, no!" cried Anna. "Look at my science project!"

Fact	Inference		
○	○	**4. A.**	Anna made a model volcano.
○	○	**B.**	On Friday Anna overslept.
○	○	**C.**	Anna dropped her science project.
○	○	**D.**	Anna was late for school.

---

5. Ramón smelled the flowers he had brought with him to the tutoring session. He quickly hid them behind his back when Mrs. Jenkins came into the room. Mrs. Jenkins had been tutoring him in English for the past year, and today was the last session. As Mrs. Jenkins sat down, Ramón surprised her with the bouquet.

Fact	Inference		
○	○	**5. A.**	Ramón wanted to thank Mrs. Jenkins.
○	○	**B.**	Mrs. Jenkins was Ramón's tutor.
○	○	**C.**	Ramón is thoughtful.
○	○	**D.**	Mrs. Jenkins did not expect the flowers.

Writing Roundup

Read each story. Then read the question that follows it. Write your answer on the lines below each question.

1. Juanita copied the exact way Sammy Sosa positioned his feet. She had examined pictures of him standing by the plate for the Chicago Cubs. She also copied the exact way he positioned his powerful hands on a bat. Standing there and looking out toward the mound, she knew she was ready.

What is Juanita doing?

_____

_____

2. Nicholas congratulated himself. He kept his old aid for a spare in case of an emergency. Now his new aid wasn't working. He quickly removed it. Then he fixed his spare aid in place in his ear. It worked perfectly. He hadn't missed much of the movie.

What was Nicholas doing?

_____

_____

3. Moving rapidly through aisle 1, Keisha sees soups in packages and in many different size cans. In aisle 2, she sees frozen foods, including vegetables and fruits. Upon reaching aisle 3, she sees envelopes, magazines, and many greeting cards.

Where is Keisha?

_____

_____

Read the paragraph below. Then answer the questions.

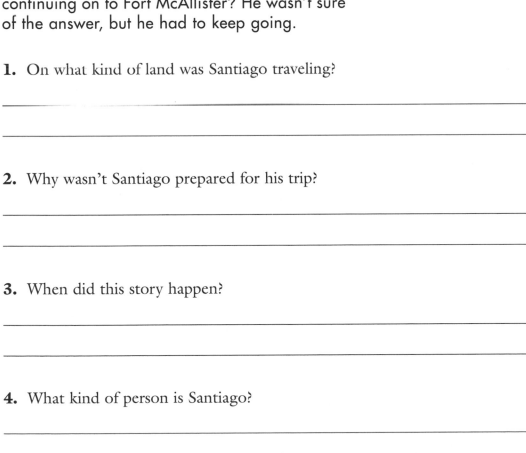

Santiago had been riding for six hours. He guessed it would still be a few hours before the blazing sun went down. His faithful horse was thirsty. He could tell by the way the horse's breathing sounded. Along the way, Santiago hadn't noticed any signs of water. There weren't even many cactuses. There was what seemed like an ocean of sand and an occasional rock. He was thirsty too, and he suspected he was beginning to sound like his poor horse. Was he capable of continuing on to Fort McAllister? He wasn't sure of the answer, but he had to keep going.

1. On what kind of land was Santiago traveling?

_____

_____

2. Why wasn't Santiago prepared for his trip?

_____

_____

3. When did this story happen?

_____

_____

4. What kind of person is Santiago?

_____

_____

Check Yourself

Unit 1

What Are Facts?

p. 6

Fact: December 1903

Fact: Orville Wright

Practice Finding Facts

p. 7

3. B

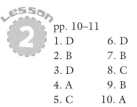**LESSON 1** pp. 8–9

1. B	6. B
2. C	7. A
3. A	8. C
4. C	9. A
5. D	10. D

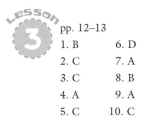**LESSON 2** pp. 10–11

1. D	6. D
2. B	7. B
3. D	8. C
4. A	9. B
5. C	10. A

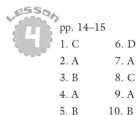**LESSON 3** pp. 12–13

1. B	6. D
2. C	7. A
3. C	8. B
4. A	9. A
5. C	10. C

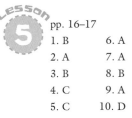**LESSON 4** pp. 14–15

1. C	6. D
2. A	7. A
3. B	8. C
4. A	9. A
5. B	10. B

LESSON 5 pp. 16–17

1. B	6. A
2. A	7. A
3. B	8. B
4. C	9. A
5. C	10. D

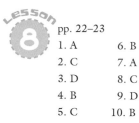**LESSON 6** pp. 18–19

1. A	6. B
2. A	7. A
3. B	8. C
4. D	9. C
5. D	10. C

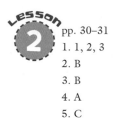**LESSON 7** pp. 20–21

1. D	6. B
2. C	7. A
3. A	8. C
4. D	9. C
5. B	10. B

**LESSON 8** pp. 22–23

1. A	6. B
2. C	7. A
3. D	8. C
4. B	9. D
5. C	10. B

Writing Roundup

p. 24

Possible answers include:

1. The Statue of Liberty is a figure of a robed woman holding a torch.

2. France gave the statue to the United States as a gift.

3. The statue is 151 feet tall.

p. 25

Check that you have four facts in your paragraph.

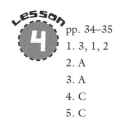

Unit 2

What Is Sequence?

p. 26

2, 3, 1

Practice with Sequence

p. 27

3. B

**LESSON 1** pp. 28–29

1. 2, 3, 1	
2. B	
3. B	
4. B	
5. C	

LESSON 2 pp. 30–31

1. 1, 2, 3	
2. B	
3. B	
4. A	
5. C	

LESSON 3 pp. 32–33

1. 2, 3, 1	
2. A	
3. B	
4. B	
5. C	

LESSON 4 pp. 34–35

1. 3, 1, 2	
2. A	
3. A	
4. C	
5. C	

LESSON 5 pp. 36–37

1. 2, 3, 1	
2. A	
3. A	
4. C	
5. A	

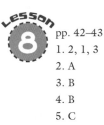**LESSON 6** pp. 38–39

1. 1, 3, 2	
2. A	
3. C	
4. C	
5. C	

LESSON 7 pp. 40–41

1. 3, 1, 2	
2. A	
3. C	
4. C	
5. B	

LESSON 8 pp. 42–43

1. 2, 1, 3	
2. A	
3. B	
4. B	
5. C	

Writing Roundup

p. 44

Possible answers include:

1. The first thing Janet does is strap on spurs and loop a rope around a tree.

2. Janet ties herself to the tree when she reaches the nest.

3. Janet clamps the band on after she has slowly pulled the eagle close.

4. A baby eagle might jump from the nest if it has been frightened.

p. 45

Check that your paragraph is written in sequence.

Check that you have used time order words, such as first, next, and last.

Unit 3

Working with Context

p. 47

2. B
3. D

LESSON 1 pp. 48–49

1. B   9. B
2. D   10. B
3. A   11. D
4. B   12. D
5. D   13. B
6. C   14. C
7. D   15. C
8. A   16. B

LESSON 2 pp. 50–51

1. D   9. D
2. B   10. C
3. C   11. A
4. A   12. B
5. D   13. B
6. A   14. C
7. B   15. C
8. A   16. A

LESSON 3 pp. 52–53

1. C   9. C
2. C   10. D
3. C   11. B
4. A   12. A
5. A   13. C
6. B   14. A
7. C   15. B
8. D   16. D

LESSON 4 pp. 54–55

1. C   9. D
2. B   10. C
3. C   11. A
4. B   12. B
5. D   13. A
6. C   14. C
7. A   15. A
8. C   16. D

LESSON 5 pp. 56–57

1. B   5. B
2. C   6. C
3. D   7. A
4. A   8. A

LESSON 6 pp. 58–59

1. B   5. B
2. D   6. C
3. B   7. B
4. D   8. B

LESSON 7 pp. 60–61

1. C   5. B
2. D   6. D
3. C   7. C
4. D   8. A

LESSON 8 pp. 62–63

1. B   5. C
2. C   6. A
3. B   7. D
4. C   8. B

Writing Roundup

p. 64

Possible answers include:

1. game or party
2. pizza or tacos
3. neighborhood or world
4. welcome or comfortable
5. clouds or city
6. toys or ants

p. 65

Possible answers include

1. It might be an elephant.
   It might be a lion.

2. A baby giraffe was eating leaves.
   Some chimps were eating
   bananas.

3. He shot a whole roll of film.
   He took many pictures.

4. They talked about making
   banners. They talked about
   getting old photos of the city.

5. They might do a play. They
   might have a band concert.

6. She suggested fireworks.
   She suggested a parade.

Unit 4

Practice Finding the Main Idea

p. 67

The correct answer is C.
The paragraph tells about the
ways in which microchips are
used in wristwatches, computers,
robots, video games, and
space shuttles.

LESSON 1 pp. 68–69

1. B
2. D
3. D
4. C
5. D

LESSON 2 pp. 70–71

1. D
2. A
3. C
4. C
5. B

LESSON 3 pp. 72–73

1. B
2. C
3. C
4. C
5. D

LESSON 4 pp. 74–75

1. B
2. D
3. B
4. A
5. A

LESSON 5 pp. 76–77

1. C
2. C
3. C
4. C
5. B

LESSON 6 pp. 78–79

1. C
2. C
3. A
4. D
5. A

LESSON 7 pp. 80–81

1. C
2. C
3. B
4. D
5. A

LESSON 8 pp. 82–83

1. B
2. C
3. C
4. C
5. A

Writing Roundup

p. 84

Possible answers include:

1. Pigs used to search for
   truffles in France.

2. Men used to wear masks and
   dance women's parts in ballets.

3. Matzeliger invented the
   shoe–shaping machine.

p. 85

Check that you have
underlined your main idea.

Check that you have used
four details in your story.

Unit 5

Using What You Know

p. 87

1. at a job interview
2. at a car wash
3. at a traffic light
4. on a mountain

LESSON 1 pp. 88–89

1. C
2. B
3. A
4. C
5. D

LESSON 2 pp. 90–91

1. A
2. A
3. D
4. A
5. D

LESSON 3 pp. 92–93

1. A
2. B
3. C
4. C
5. B

LESSON 4 pp. 94–95

1. A
2. C
3. D
4. A
5. B

LESSON 5 pp. 96–97

1. D
2. A
3. C
4. B
5. D

LESSON 6 pp. 98–99

1. D
2. C
3. B
4. A
5. A

LESSON 7 pp. 100–101

1. B
2. D
3. A
4. C
5. B

LESSON 8 pp. 102–103

1. B
2. D
3. D
4. C
5. C

Writing Roundup

p. 104

Possible answers include:

1. You can't play polo if you can't ride a horse.

2. Phillis Wheatley was good with languages.

3. Alonso's weather station isn't finished yet.

p. 105

Possible answers include:

1. Juneteenth is not a holiday in all states. It is celebrated only by people in Texas and in some other states.

2. There was slavery in Texas. Union troops ended slavery there.

3. Texans did not know the Civil War had ended. The Union troops told them.

4. Californians did not coin the word *Juneteenth*. People in Texas created this word.

Unit 6

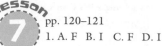

Practice Making Inferences

p. 107

2. A. F   B. I   C. I   D. F

LESSON 1 pp. 108–109

1. A. I   B. I   C. F   D. F
2. A. F   B. F   C. I   D. F
3. A. F   B. I   C. I   D. I
4. A. I   B. I   C. F   D. F
5. A. F   B. I   C. F   D. F

LESSON 2 pp. 110–111

1. A. F   B. I   C. F   D. F
2. A. F   B. I   C. I   D. I
3. A. F   B. I   C. F   D. I
4. A. I   B. F   C. I   D. F
5. A. F   B. F   C. I   D. F

LESSON 3 pp. 112–113

1. A. I   B. F   C. I   D. I
2. A. F   B. F   C. I   D. F
3. A. F   B. F   C. I   D. F
4. A. F   B. I   C. F   D. I
5. A. I   B. I   C. I   D. F

LESSON 4 pp. 114–115

1. A. F   B. I   C. F   D. I
2. A. F   B. I   C. F   D. I
3. A. I   B. F   C. F   D. I
4. A. F   B. F   C. F   D. I
5. A. F   B. I   C. I   D. F

LESSON 5 pp. 116–117

1. A. F   B. I   C. F   D. I
2. A. F   B. I   C. I   D. F
3. A. I   B. F   C. I   D. F
4. A. F   B. I   C. I   D. F
5. A. I   B. F   C. F   D. I

LESSON 6 pp. 118–119

1. A. F   B. F   C. I   D. I
2. A. I   B. I   C. I   D. F
3. A. F   B. I   C. F   D. F
4. A. F   B. F   C. F   D. I
5. A. I   B. F   C. F   D. F

LESSON 7 pp. 120–121

1. A. F   B. I   C. F   D. I
2. A. F   B. F   C. F   D. I
3. A. I   B. I   C. I   D. F
4. A. I   B. I   C. F   D. F
5. A. I   B. F   C. F   D. I

LESSON 8 pp. 122–123

1. A. F   B. F   C. I   D. F
2. A. F   B. F   C. I   D. I
3. A. I   B. F   C. F   D. I
4. A. F   B. I   C. I   D. F
5. A. I   B. F   C. I   D. I

Writing Roundup

p. 124

Possible answers include:

1. Juanita is batting in a baseball game.

2. Nicholas was changing his hearing aid because his new hearing aid wasn't working.

3. Keisha is in a grocery store or supermarket.

p. 125

Possible answers include:

1. Santiago was on a desert.

2. Santiago didn't know about the hardships on the desert. He didn't carry water with him.

3. The story probably happened in the 1800s in a time before people had cars for transportation.

4. Santiago is rugged, strong willed, and considerate.